THE
NATIONAL GALLERY
LONDON

THE
NATIONAL
GALLERY
LONDON

HOMAN POTTERTON

With a Preface by
MICHAEL LEVEY
and a complete catalogue of the paintings

345 illustrations, 75 in colour

THAMES AND HUDSON

To Michael Levey

© 1977   Thames and Hudson Ltd, London
Reprinted 1981

Printed and bound in England by Jarrold & Sons Ltd, Norwich

CONTENTS

1 An aerial view of the National Gallery with a key to the successive extensions that have been made to the building

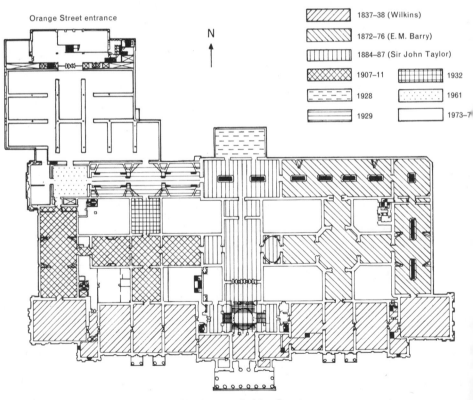

Orange Street entrance

N

1837–38 (Wilkins)	
1872–76 (E. M. Barry)	
1884–87 (Sir John Taylor)	
1907–11	1932
1928	1961
1929	1973–7

Main entrance, Trafalgar Square

PREFACE

Like the National Gallery itself, this book is good enough to need no prefacing. Still, the occasion of its publication offers an opportunity to pause and briefly consider not only what the National Gallery is but – no less pertinent today – what function it serves.

'The question of what it is, or has come to be, can hardly be answered more agreeably than by reading Homan Potterton's intelligent and steadily illuminating text, and by studying his equally intelligent choice of plates. It emerges that the National Gallery is only a collection of pictures – rather in the same way, of course, that Titian was *only* a painter or Jane Austen *only* a novelist. But it is as well to be clear on this point at a time when 'fine art' is often reduced to the status of fine print and presumed to lack the easy social-history-cum-utilitarian appeal of, say, lace-bobbins, photographs and fire-arms. Without owning any of those, the National Gallery yet manages to deserve to be called a great museum. Indeed, it has become one of the greatest picture galleries of the world, though in sheer number of works it remains one of the very smallest. Nor has it vast holdings of any one school or painter – any more than it has vast cellars of unexhibited pictures. That virtually all its 2050 or so pictures are normally on show to the public is not the least of its claims to attention.

By good fortune it began modestly, inheriting nothing (least of all a royal or nationally-based collection) and therefore having to win its way in the artistic world. It has never stopped growing, and it continues to search out and acquire masterpieces, as well as other desirable pictures. The result to date can be appreciated in the pages which follow. Such is the range of pictures that a serious book like this on the Collection becomes something of a history of Western European painting, from Duccio in Italy around 1300 up to the early twentieth century in France, and happily not only in France (as a portrait by Gustav Klimt indicates). The story is the more fascinating for being told through a concentrated series of masterpieces, giving the Collection its particular lustre and including several (like Holbein's *Ambassadors* and Velázquez's '*Rokeby*' *Venus*) unrivalled even in the collections of their painters' native countries.

Homan Potterton is conscious of the opportunities offered by these facts. He has interpreted his task not as the conventional one of sprinkling approving adjectives like literary talcum powder over major works of art but as a way of deepening understanding of them, incorporating inevitably much established knowledge but also fresh and scholarly observations (as in his discussion of Reynolds' *Banastre Tarleton*). Some lively visual juxtapositions – for example a Japanese print of ladies with parasols facing *Les Parapluies* by Renoir – testify to his unhackneyed approach and his ability to stimulate one to look again at familiar masterpieces.

That process of looking is really the essence of the Gallery's function and the justification of its existence. Nowadays we have lost the certainty of the Victorians that museums are good things, and do not seem too sure that art is necessarily a good thing. Some critics like to emphasize that a museum environment is not the natural environment for which pictures were painted. Latent puritanism worries about the accumulated 'wealth' of our museums, fearing that works of art taken from their original settings are displayed only to impress, like so much national loot or booty. Sentiment and self-interest often combine to suggest that

Old Master pictures become sterilized by being cared for and assembled for public pleasure free of charge, when they could have remained deteriorating in dark churches abroad or in country houses for which they were not painted but where one pays for the privilege of peering at them dimly between the flowering shrubs, wedding dresses, coronation chairs and silver-framed family souvenirs.

The National Gallery is not meant to serve the lost cause of nostalgia. It possesses powerful works of the imagination (caring for them physically, as Homan Potterton early reminds his readers, as well as in other ways) which deserve to be accessible to everyone and which are capable of giving sustained pleasure. Certainly, those of us lucky enough to be employed in the Gallery have increasingly to think of ways of facilitating that process, helping our visitors to relax and let their eyes gaze – without nervousness or too much awe – at what was created to give pleasure by being gazed at. Information is needed, by every one of us; and knowledge increases pleasure. Writing about the Collection happens to be only one aspect of all that the Gallery must do – is, indeed, committed to doing – but this book shows how valuable such writing can be. Its inspiration derives from an assembly of pictures which have been brought together for an important human activity: exercise of the imagination. No eye will ever exhaust the enjoyment these pictures provide, and a lifetime spent gazing at them is wisely spent.

MICHAEL LEVEY, Director

2 In the lower-floor galleries. The National Gallery is rare, if not unique, among the museums of the world in that all the paintings in the Collection are on permanent exhibition. There are no 'cellars' and no undiscovered or neglected masterpieces

3 The main façade of the National Gallery towards the north side of Trafalgar Square. It was designed by William Wilkins and completed in 1838

HISTORY OF THE COLLECTION

The National Gallery was founded in 1824 when the government purchased for £57,000 thirty-eight paintings from the collection of the late John Julius Angerstein, a Russian émigré banker who had lived in London and who died in 1823. The Gallery was first opened to the public in Angerstein's former town house, 100 Pall Mall, on 10 May 1824. Shortly before the government's purchase of the Angerstein pictures, Sir George Beaumont and the Rev. William Holwell Carr had promised to give their important collections of paintings to the nation if a suitable building was provided to house them; and in 1836 and 1831 respectively the Beaumont and Holwell Carr pictures joined those of Angerstein in the new National Gallery. Unlike most of the great national collections of Europe, therefore, England's National Gallery is not built upon the foundations of a former royal collection, but is one which has been assembled over a period of more than 150 years by purchases reflecting the tastes of successive Directors, and by the generous gifts and bequests of private individuals. As the National Gallery has always seen it as its duty to retain in this country masterpieces of paintings which have often long been in the possession of English families,

it has become a treasure house of the nation's heritage.

The pictures purchased and presented in the Gallery's first years were very much what one would expect in any late eighteenth-or early nineteenth-century English collection. Many of them had recently been imported from revolutionary Europe and came from the palaces of dispossessed French and Italian aristocrats. The enormous Sebastiano del Piombo (No. 1 in the National Gallery inventory), two *Groups of Heads* after Correggio and two supposed paintings by the Carracci had come from the celebrated collection of the Dukes of Orleans; and all five paintings by Claude in the Angerstein collection had also come out of France. Most of Angerstein's pictures, which included Raphael's *Pope Julius II* (p. 78), were Italian of the sixteenth and seventeenth centuries; but the collection also numbered paintings by Cuyp and Rembrandt, Rubens and Van Dyck and some English pictures including *Lord Heathfield* by Reynolds (page 142) and Hogarth's much-loved series *Marriage à la Mode* (pages 146 and 147).

Sir George Beaumont's collection was small, just sixteen in number, but choice. There were three more Claudes, a further Rembrandt,

9

Rubens's *Château de Steen* (page 100) and one of the National Gallery's most famous paintings, *The Stonemason's Yard* by Canaletto (page 133). Many of the Gallery's small collection of Italian seventeenth-century paintings came with the Holwell Carr bequest in 1831: three by Domenichino as well as pictures by Mola, Guercino and Annibale Carracci. Holwell Carr also bequeathed paintings by Rembrandt, Rubens, Titian and Tintoretto.

Within the first decade of its existence, therefore, the National Collection had taken shape, and in the same period the Trustees also made some independent purchases. In their choice of painting they favoured the work of Titian (*Bacchus and Ariadne*, page 80), Annibale Carracci (*Domine, Quo Vadis?*) and Correggio (*Mercury instructing Cupid*, page 73, and the *Madonna of the Basket*): in other words, the work of painters already for the most part represented in the Gallery. It was Lord Farnborough, one of the early Trustees, who came nearest to formulating such purchasing policy as existed in these early years when he said that 'it was a great point to obtain the best works of any considerable master'; the main objectives of the purchasing policy, he argued, should be limited 'to the works of Raphael, Correggio and Titian . . . which . . . must be obtained whenever the opportunity presents itself'. This policy seems indeed to have governed the purchases made by the Trustees for almost the first thirty years of the Gallery's existence. By 1853, when a House of Commons Select Committee made an Inquiry into the affairs of the Gallery (an Inquiry which led to the appointment of the first Director in 1855), the Trustees had further purchased three paintings each by Raphael, Rubens and Guido Reni, two each by Rembrandt and Van Eyck, a Titian, Bellini's *Doge* (page 49) and the *Boar Hunt* by Velázquez. All of these, with the exception of Titian's *Tribute Money*, came from English private collections.

By the middle of the century, however, museum taste both in this country and elsewhere was changing in favour of a more historical approach to collecting; and it was felt desirable that the National Gallery should be 'a complete historical collection' meaning that 'it must commence from the time of Giotto'. Not only were pictures by Italian painters earlier than Raphael now sought but also those by early German and Netherlandish artists; and in 1854 the Trustees purchased twenty-seven pictures predominantly by early German masters from the Krüger collection in Germany.

In 1855 Sir Charles Eastlake was appointed the first Director of the Gallery and in the ten years of his directorship, when he had absolute authority in the choice of acquisitions, he bought many outstanding early Italian pictures. Piero della Francesca was an artist newly 'discovered' in the mid-nineteenth century, and Eastlake bought a masterpiece by him, *The Baptism of Christ* (page 33), for £241 in 1861. Appreciation of Botticelli was similarly in its infancy but Eastlake purchased three pictures by him – two of these are now catalogued as 'Studio' – while a fourth was actually bought as a Masaccio but is now accepted as Botticelli. Other triumphant acquisitions by Eastlake, who travelled annually in Italy in pursuit of possible purchases, were *The Martyrdom of St Sebastian* by the brothers Pollaiuolo (page 35) for £3,155 in 1857; an altarpiece by Mantegna; a triptych by Duccio; three paintings by Crivelli; the ever-popular *Rout of San Romano* by Uccello (page 30) and *Mythological Subject* by Piero di Cosimo (page 138).

Eastlake's taste for the 'Primitives', as the early Italian painters were called, reflected contemporary taste in England. Classical architecture had largely given way to Gothic, classical ornament to medieval, and in painting itself several artists turned to these same early Italians for inspiration; attempts were even made to transplant the Italian technique of fresco painting into England. The Director's taste was shared by Prince Albert, who also exerted through patronage, both official and private, a strong influence on the arts in his adopted country. The Prince also collected pictures, mainly 'Primitives', and in 1863 Queen Victoria presented a group of important early Netherlandish, German and Italian paintings to the National Gallery at his wish.

Thus by 1865, when Eastlake died, the Italian schools of the fifteenth and sixteenth centuries were well represented, as also were the earlier Northern schools of painting, and the great painters of the seventeenth century, Claude, Poussin, Rembrandt, Rubens and Van Dyck.

Although Dutch pictures had been collected in England from the middle of the eighteenth century, Eastlake seems to have felt little affinity with them, and indeed throughout his entire directorate he bought only three Dutch pictures, all by members of the Ruisdael family. But some private collectors in England at the time were buying Dutch seventeenth-century paintings, and two of the greatest collections,

4 The gallery of seventeenth-century French paintings

those of Sir Robert Peel and Wynn Ellis, came to the Gallery in 1871 and 1876 respectively. The former, which was purchased by the Trustees, numbered seventy-seven pictures including three by Cuyp, two by De Hoogh and the famous *Avenue, Middelharnis* by Hobbema (page 117). Rubens's *Chapeau de Paille* (page 101) was also a Peel collection picture. Of the pictures in the Wynn Ellis bequest the Trustees accepted ninety-four including a splendid large Cuyp and several by Van der Heyden and Godfried Schalcken. Wynn Ellis also bequeathed the *Portrait of a Man* by Bouts (page 58) and the *Tax-gatherers* by Marinus (page 60). Within five years, therefore (1871–6), another great school of European painting came to be remarkably represented at the National Gallery; and in 1910 this was further augmented by the bequest of George Salting – the largest bequest ever: it numbered 192 pictures, including six by Jan Steen, three each by Van der Neer and Van Goyen and others by the Ruisdaels. An important item in the Salting bequest was the *Virgin and Child before a Firescreen* by Robert Campin (page 50).

The best known of all Italian eighteenth-century painters, Canaletto, had been repre-

sented at the National Gallery almost from its foundation: Sir George Beaumont's gift included *The Stonemason's Yard* (page 133), and Wynn Ellis also bequeathed three important paintings by this artist. It was, however, the third Director, Sir Frederick Burton, who laid the foundations of what is now a representative eighteenth-century Italian collection. In ten years, between 1881 and 1891, he purchased several paintings by Giovanni Battista and Giovanni Domenico Tiepolo, Zais and Pietro Longhi, including the *Exhibition of a Rhinoceros at Venice* (page 135). Many of Burton's other acquisitions were outstanding, and as he was Director at a time when changes in English legislation meant that pictures hitherto held in trust might be sold, several of his important purchases were from long-established English collections. The more remarkable were: *The Virgin of the Rocks* by Leonardo (page 69); *Philip IV in Brown and Silver* by Velázquez (page 104); *The Ambassadors* by Holbein (page 64); *Charles I on Horseback* by Van Dyck (page 104); *The Ansidei Madonna* by Raphael (page 79); *The Origin of the Milky Way* by Tintoretto (page 88); and the four *Allegories* by Veronese (page 86). Burton also purchased, in 1892, the Gallery's

5 Holbein's *Ambassadors* (see page 64) hangs in one of the rooms added to the building in 1975

first Vermeer: *A Young Woman standing at a Virginal* (page 125) – a picture which had originally been in the collection of Etienne Théophile Burger, whose researches 'discovered' and rehabilitated Vermeer in the late nineteenth century.

During the nineteenth century the Trustees purchased no contemporary painting by a foreign artist and it was not until the bequest of Sir Hugh Lane in 1917 that the Gallery acquired its first examples of many of the great nineteenth-century French painters, including Manet, Monet, Renoir, Pissarro and Degas. Among the Lane pictures Renoir's *Les Parapluies* (page 163) is outstanding. A fund, established by Samuel Courtauld in 1924 for the purchase of late nineteenth-century French paintings, has resulted in many important acquisitions, not least *La La* by Degas (page 164), Seurat's enormous *Bathers, Asnières* (page 168) and two paintings by Cézanne.

Many outstanding purchases this century, including *The Rokeby Venus* by Velázquez (page 108), Holbein's *Christina of Denmark* (page 63) and the Leonardo Cartoon (page 71), have been made possible only with the help of the National Art-Collections Fund, an independent body set up in 1903 to prevent the export of works of art of outstanding merit. In 1956 an Act of Parliament gave the Chancellor of the Exchequer the authority to accept works of art in lieu of Estate Duty, and this Act has resulted in the acquisition by the Gallery of

Memlinc's *'Donne' Triptych* (page 56) and the double portrait by Jordaens (page 102). Current legislation also makes the sale of works of art by private treaty to national museums attractive to potential sellers, as such transactions are exempt from all taxes; Rembrandt's portrait of Hendrickje Stoffels (page 112) was bought in 1976 with mutual benefits to both seller and the Gallery.

After the opening of the Tate Gallery in 1897 many of the more modern paintings, both British and foreign, were transferred there, and the Tate is now the home of the national collection of modern foreign art and of British painting. As a result of these transfers the National Gallery collection is now a relatively small one with no more than about two thousand paintings, predominantly Old Masters.

The building in which the collection is housed has been continuously enlarged with the years. For its first fourteen years it had to exist in temporary accommodation, first in Angerstein's former town house, and later in a neighbouring building in Pall Mall. It was not until 1838 that the Gallery in Trafalgar Square, designed by William Wilkins (1778–1839) specifically as a National Gallery, was opened. Since that date, although Wilkins's long façade remains substantially the same, many extra exhibition rooms have been added to the north of the original gallery. In 1939 the pictures were exiled for safety to Wales, returning after the War. The latest extension was in 1975 when thirteen new rooms were added, and now, perhaps uniquely among the museums of the world, the National Gallery has sufficient space to exhibit its entire collection.

Since World War II most of the pictures now exhibited on the main floor have been cleaned in the Gallery's own conservation studios. In conjunction with a programme of conservation, photographic and scientific departments have also been developed. The latter conducts research into the conditions in which pictures should ideally be exhibited and analyses the pigments used by the painters in different places and at different periods. A framing shop within the Gallery maintains and sometimes renews frames, many of which are as old as the paintings which they contain. But in recent years perhaps the Gallery's most remarkable achievement is the publication of detailed catalogues of all the pictures in the collection, catalogues which have served as models for museums throughout the world; and it is from these publications that much of the information contained in this book has been obtained.

6 The framing department. The large frame on the left is being prepared for *The Vendramin Family* by Titian (see page 81)

7 One of the conservation studios

CONSERVATION TECHNIQUES

The structure of paintings

None of the pictures in the National Gallery, nor indeed any pictures anywhere, can be regarded as just a coloured surface. A painting is a structure built up of a series of stratified layers. The basic 'layer' is called the *support,* which in the case of most National Gallery pictures is either wood, canvas or copper. In general most earlier paintings have wooden supports. In Italy poplar was most often used, but from the sixteenth century canvas became more common, except in seventeenth-century Holland, where wood and copper panels were almost universally employed. Rubens also frequently painted on wood.

The word 'canvas' is used to describe a variety of woven fabrics upon which pictures

are painted. The canvas is stretched on a wooden frame called a *stretcher.* The immediate advantage of canvas over wood as a support is that it is so much lighter and as a result can be used for much larger paintings. It is also much less susceptible to damage caused by variation in atmospheric conditions; but as it is also much less rigid as a support it can be torn and the paint is more likely to crack or flake off.

On top of the support is laid the *ground,* a smooth layer of plaster or paint. This ground is often white, but some painters used other colours, for example Poussin in the seventeenth century used a red ground. The picture itself, which may have been preceded by a preliminary drawing, is painted on this ground and often consists of several layers of paint which may show changes made by the artist as he worked on the picture. When such changes are visible on the surface of the picture, they are called *pentimenti.* The paint consists of *pigment,* which is a coloured powder, and *medium,* the material used to bind the powder. Pigments vary considerably in their origin. Some of them are taken from the earth, some, such as lead white and cobalt blue, are synthetic preparations, and some are based on dyes which generally derive from plants. It is now often possible to date a picture approximately on the basis of an analysis of the pigments it contains, for in the case of most pigments it is known when and where they were used. The medium used to bind the pigment also varies. In many of the earlier Italian pictures, the medium is egg which, when mixed with the pigment, produces what is called *egg tempera.* From the fifteenth century onwards drying oils are the medium most consistently employed by painters throughout Europe. Finally, the top 'layer' of a painting is a clear *varnish* which, in addition to protecting the paint surface, helps show the true brilliance of the colours.

Types of deterioration in a painting

Change or deterioration in any one or all of the several strata of a picture can be brought about by a variety of means; and when it happens in the National Gallery the picture is treated in the Gallery's own conservation studios.

8 The back of a picture painted on canvas showing the stretcher

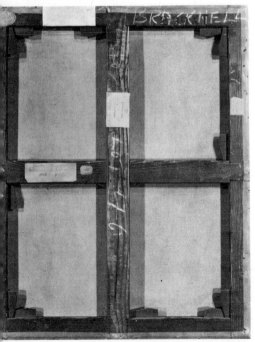

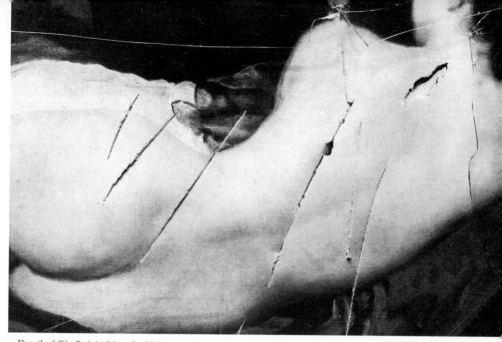

9 Detail of *The Rokeby Venus* by Velázquez (compare page 108). This photograph shows the picture after it had been slashed by a suffragette in 1914. The fine breaks near the top of the photograph are in the glass only

The most dramatic change that can take place in a picture is when it is maliciously damaged. Fortunately this happens only very rarely, but it did happen in 1914 when Velázquez's *Rokeby Venus* (page 108) was slashed by a suffragette (9). Accidental damage can also occur, as for example in the case of Delaroche's *Execution of Lady Jane Grey* (page 155), which was damaged when the Thames flooded the lower floors of the Tate Gallery, where it was stored in 1928. Change or deterioration in a picture may also be caused because of the nature of the materials used by the artist. Several paintings by Reynolds, including *Lord Heathfield* (page 142), have an unsightly surface 'cracking' which is caused by the dark bitumen which the artist used in his paint to give his picture a richer overall effect. Most pictures become dark with age as a result of the discolouration of the natural resin in the varnish which protects the paint (10). A picture may also be affected by the environment in which it hangs. A painting on a wood panel may warp or crack as a result of being kept in too dry an atmosphere, although, as more and more rooms in the National Gallery are air-conditioned, this type of damage can be avoided by controlling the atmosphere.

10 *Portrait of Hendrickje Stoffels* by Rembrandt (compare page 112). This photograph was taken during cleaning when the discoloured surface varnish had been removed from most of the left-hand side of the painting, and also from a small spot bottom right

15

Pictures can also be substantially altered by the efforts of past restorers, who probably worked with the best intentions. In repairing a damaged area a restorer might have repainted a larger area than was necessary in order to 'blend in' his restoration with the original paint. He might also have 'improved' a picture by painting out or changing an area of the composition (13). Other improvements might include the application of judicious draperies and fig-leaves in areas which were at one time considered indecent (11).

The simplest form of change that may take place in any picture is that it just becomes dirty as a result of the natural accretion of dirt and grime only to be expected in a gallery which is in the centre of a very large city.

13 (opposite) Detail of *Sts Fabian and Sebastian* by Giovanni di Paolo. This photograph was taken when a rectangular area of the picture (right) had been cleaned revealing that at some time a restorer had enlarged the form of St Sebastian's arm. Presumably his intention was to 'improve' the picture and at the same time repair the damage at the saint's wrist

11 (above) Detail of *An Allegory* by Bronzino (compare page 72). This photograph, taken before the cleaning of the picture, shows the drapery and leaves which had been painted, in the interests of modesty, over the body and buttocks of Venus and Cupid respectively

12 X-ray photograph of a detail from *The Virgin and Child before a firescreen* by Robert Campin (compare page 50). The modern part of the picture can readily be distinguished on the right by the greater opacity of the paint in that area. The white streaks are worm holes which have been filled with white lead

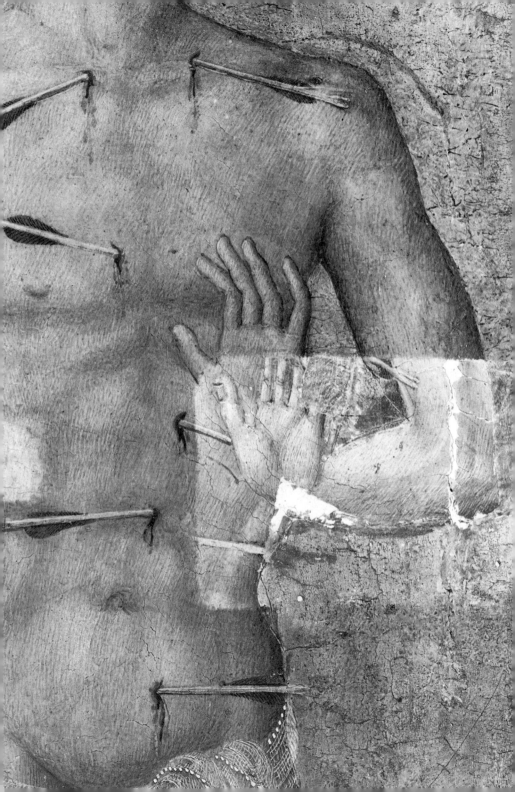

14 *The Nativity* by Piero della Francesca. This photograph, taken under raking light, shows how the wooden panel on which the picture is painted is extensively warped

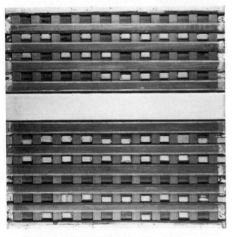

15 The back of *The Nativity* by Piero della Francesca which in the past has been 'cradled' in an attempt to prevent the picture warping

Conservation of the support

Pictures painted on panel are more susceptible to damage caused by the environment in which they are kept than are paintings on canvas. This arises out of the fact that one side of the wood panel is 'sealed' by the paint of the picture while the back is free to absorb or lose moisture with any changes in the relative humidity of the atmosphere. As it does so the panel will expand or contract at right angles to the grain of the wood, and may warp and eventually crack. More often than not, however, a panel will crack because of the attempts made in the past to prevent its warping. These attempts included '*cradling*' or '*buttoning*' the back of the panel. '*Cradling*' (15) consists of wooden battens glued parallel to the grain of the panel at intervals across it. Free-running slats were inserted across these battens with the intention that they should allow some movement of the panel while preventing it warping badly. Invariably these runners became jammed which resulted in the panel cracking. '*Buttons*' (17) are tiny squares of wood glued along a join at the back of a cracked panel. In modern conservation it is the practice to remove any restrictions previously applied to the back of a panel and to allow movement, while attempting at the same time to keep it to a minimum by maintaining the picture in as stable atmospheric conditions as possible. When a panel is excessively warped it may be treated by placing it, picture upwards, on a framework over dampened pads. The back of the panel absorbs the moisture which it has lost, and the picture flattens. Where a panel is cracked the two pieces are joined as simply as possible by glueing the two edges to each other. Worm may also cause damage to pictures on panel, but this is easily treated by the use of suitable insecticides. Badly eaten panels may be consolidated with a wax cement.

Most paintings on canvas which are older than the nineteenth century have at some time been *lined*; that is, a new canvas has been stuck to the back of the original one in order to strengthen it. When this process is repeated it is called '*re-lining*'. In order to carry out a lining the picture is removed from its stretcher and a new canvas coated with adhesive is attached to the back of the original canvas. Traditionally, when this is done, the picture is ironed from the back in order to force the adhesive through the original canvas and into the ground of the painting. The type of adhesive used varies: it can be a flour paste mixed with glue or alternatively a wax-resin mixture. In the case of a wax-resin, it melts with ironing and permeates more readily through the old canvas and ground and fixes from the back any loose particles of paint. More recently a method of lining has been developed which involves the use of a specially designed hot-table (18). The picture is placed, surface upwards, together with its lining canvas and wax-resin under a thin membrane on the hot-table. A vacuum is created under the membrane which draws the painting and lining together while at the same time the table is heated so that the wax melts and the two canvasses are evenly joined.

16 A picture on panel which has warped. Photograph taken before treatment of the panel

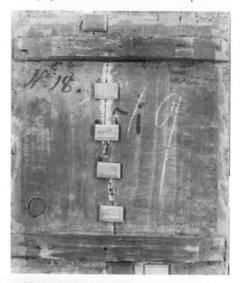

17 The back of a picture painted on a wooden panel which has cracked. 'Buttons' have been applied to mend the crack

18 *St Zenobius revives a Dead Boy* by Bilivert during relining on a hot-table

19 *The Martyrdom of St Stephen*
attributed to Antonio Carracci, before
cleaning

20 x-ray photograph of *The Martyrdom
of St Stephen* showing the figures of God
the Father and Christ, not visible in the
painting, in the top left-hand corner.
The x-ray also shows that the
composition was begun the other way
up: the figures of the saint and the right-
hand man stoning him are visible in the
area occupied by the sky in the finished
picture

21 An engraving of *The Martyrdom of St Stephen* made in 1812 before the figures of God the Father and Christ had been painted out

22 (below) *The Martyrdom of St Stephen* after cleaning when the overpaint was removed to reveal the figures in the sky (top left)

23 Detail of the *Pietà* by Zoppo showing the discoloured retouchings on Christ's body

Conservation of the paint surface

Most of the steps taken to conserve the support of a picture, as described above, also help generally to make the paint surface more secure; but small areas of *flaking* or *blistering* paint can be secured much more simply. Blisters are treated by allowing a suitable adhesive to seep from the picture surface under the raised paint and then the paint is pressed down with a warm spatula until it sticks in place. Paint losses are painted back by the restorer using pigments mixed with synthetic resins which will in future be easily removable. As a general principle the 'restoration' should be recognizable at close proximity but be at the same time sufficiently convincing so as not to detract from the overall effect of the picture.

The cleaning of pictures

There are three different stages in the cleaning of a picture, but not all pictures require the restorer to proceed to the second or third. First of all the dirt on the surface of the painting is removed; then the old varnish, which is probably discoloured. Finally the restorer will carefully remove any old retouchings. All these processes are carried out using appropriate solvents or in some circumstances scalpels. The removal of old retouchings is the most difficult task, as caution must be exercised in determining the extent of the retouchings, and also the wisdom in removing them; they may sometimes be more 'convincing' than those a restorer will be able to re-create.

Many old retouchings are perfectly obvious even to the naked eye, as the technique of the earlier restorer will be at such variance with that of the artist. Retouchings may also have darkened (23) through some chemical change in the paint used, and so will no longer match in colour the surrounding area. More rarely retouchings fade or bleach. Sometimes an engraving or old copy of a picture will exist which shows the composition in a different state, and from that it will be possible to determine the extent of the retouched areas. In the case of *The Martyrdom of St Stephen*, attributed to Antonio Carracci, an engraving of 1812 (21) showed the figures of God the Father and Christ in the top left-hand corner of

24 Detail of 'The Arnolfini Marriage' by Jan van Eyck (compare page 52). This photograph, taken in infra-red light, shows the artist's drawing of an earlier position for the hand which he later abandoned and painted over

the picture; but these figures had been painted out (probably when the picture was owned by a clergyman, the Rev. William Holwell Carr) and were only revealed when the picture was cleaned.

Technical aids to the examination of pictures
Retouchings may also be spotted by the use of an *ultra-violet light,* which excites different types and degrees of fluorescence in different substances, but provides information only about the very surface of a painting. Thus retouchings fluoresce differently from original paint, usually appearing as dark spots, and old varnish fluoresces with a lemon-yellow colour. *Infra-red* radiation will penetrate a little deeper than ultra-violet and, particularly in the case of earlier pictures where the paint is often very thinly applied, an infra-red photograph may show up the artist's original drawing (24). A variation between the original design and the visible picture, however, need not necessarily be due to the retouchings of a later restorer, but may well represent, as in the case of Van Eyck's *Arnolfini Marriage,* a change made by the artist

himself. *X-radiography* is probably the technique which shows the most dramatic results when applied to a picture (20 and pages 45, 73, 82, 91). The rays, which are directed through the picture on to a photographic plate, are absorbed according to the density of the pigments and other material they pass through. White lead, which was used in practically all pictures from the Middle Ages to the nineteenth century, is the densest pigment, so that on an X-ray photograph areas of a picture containing white lead will show lightest and areas with little or no dense paint will show dark. Holes in the picture will show black. As the rays register the sum of all the superimposed layers of a picture, features of the support and ground are visible, together with any changes in the composition which the artist made during the execution of a picture.

During the cleaning and restoration of any picture at the National Gallery all the stages in the process are recorded by photographs which are then used to form a 'Conservation Dossier' on the picture. As a general principle nothing is done which in future cannot be reversed.

BIBLIOGRAPHY

All the pictures in the Gallery are described in full in the following
National Gallery catalogues:

The Earlier Italian Schools by Martin Davies. Second Edition (revised) 1961

The Early Netherlandish School by Martin Davies. Third Edition (revised)
1968.

The German School by Michael Levey. 1959

The Sixteenth-Century Italian Schools by Cecil Gould. 1975

The Seventeenth and Eighteenth Century Italian Schools by Michael Levey. 1971

The Dutch School by Neil Maclaren. 1960

The Flemish School, circa 1600–circa 1900 by Gregory Martin. 1970

The Spanish School by Neil Maclaren. Second Edition, revised, by Allan
Braham. 1970

The French School by Martin Davies. Second Edition (revised) 1957

The British School by Martin Davies. Second Edition (revised) 1959

The French School, Early 19th century, Impressionists, Post-Impressionists etc. by
Martin Davies with additions and some revisions by Cecil Gould. 1970

The author is indebted to Dr. N. B. Penny who suggested the possible
derivation of Banastre Tarleton's pose in the portrait by Reynolds (page 141)

FRENCH SCHOOL (*c.* 1395 or later)
Richard II presented to the Virgin and Child
by his Patron Saints
('The Wilton Diptych')
Each panel 45.7 × 29.2 cm

The Diptych is so called because it was for long at Wilton House, the seat of the Earls of Pembroke, from where it was purchased by the Gallery in 1929. Before that it was in the collection of Charles I. Made to fold like a book, it is clearly portable. The outside, which is damaged, is painted with the arms of Edward the Confessor (King of England, d. 1066) impaled with those of the Kingdom on one side and a white hart 'lodged' (the badge of Richard II) on the other. The inside shows Richard II presented to the Virgin and Child by his patron saints, and is remarkably well preserved. Richard II (1367–1400) became King of England at the age of ten and was deposed in 1399.

Armorial details in the picture suggest that it cannot have been painted before 1395. On one side Richard is shown in his youth, kneeling, with his hands open in expectation. His robe is richly embroidered with a pattern of white

harts encircled by collars of broom-cods. Such collars were French and associated in particular with the French King Charles VI whose daughter, Isabella, Richard married in 1396. Behind the kneeling King stand St John the Baptist, St Edward the Confessor (with a ring) and St Edmund, King and Martyr. The other side shows the Virgin accompanied by eleven angels. While Richard kneels in an earthly landscape with trees in the background, the Virgin and her host stand in a more 'heavenly' bed of flowers. The angels are personal to Richard: they wear his badge and also collars of broom-cods. The Christ Child, whose halo is ornamented with a Crown of Thorns and the Nails of the Passion, gestures, possibly in benediction or alternatively towards the banner held by one of the angels. The banner, a red cross on a white ground, was the flag of England at one time; it was also the banner of Christ's Resurrection, and a flag associated with crusades.

The significance of many of the details in the painting remains in doubt, and so does the use or meaning of the Diptych itself. Its origin is also uncertain. It is possibly English, more probably French, but painted in a style that is known as International Gothic.

DUCCIO (active 1278, d. 1319)
The Annunciation and *Jesus opens the Eyes of a Man born blind*
43.2 × 43.8 cm and 43.2 × 45.1 cm

These two pictures are predella panels from Duccio's masterwork, the high altarpiece of Siena Cathedral, which the artist contracted to paint 'with his own hand' on 9 October 1308 and which was placed in the Cathedral on 9 June 1311. Called the *Maestà* (a generic term for an altarpiece which showed the Virgin and Child enthroned in majesty), the altarpiece was painted on both back and front. *The Annunciation* is from the front, which also contained other scenes from the early life of Christ. The reverse showed scenes from His ministry, including the episode in St John's Gospel where Christ, followed by the twelve Apostles, gave sight at the Pool of Siloam to a beggar born blind. Most of the other parts of the altarpiece are in the Cathedral museum, Siena.

Ascribed to GIOTTO (1266?–1337)
Pentecost
45.7 × 43.8 cm

Giotto, who was Florentine, is generally regarded as the founder of modern painting. This panel is from a series which may have decorated a cupboard door in some sacristy. It may be Giotto's own work or, more probably, executed in his studio. The subject of the picture is taken from the Acts of the Apostles.

The Twelve stand in an enclosed space with tongues of fire on their heads, while outside the multitude marvel, each man hearing the Apostles speak in his own language.

Working in the first decades of the fourteenth century, Giotto gave his paintings a naturalism and 'reality' which contrasted with the Byzantine-inspired paintings of his contemporaries; and the innovations which the artist made did not become commonplace in Italy for another hundred years.

GIOVANNI DI PAOLO (active 1420, d. 1482)
Two predella panels from an altarpiece:
St John the Baptist retiring to the Desert and
The Baptism of Christ
31.1 × 38.8 cm and 30.8 × 44.5 cm

These two panels, together with two others
also in the National Gallery, are predella panels
from an altarpiece the original location of
which is not known. The scene of the *Baptism
of Christ* is derived closely from a relief,
installed in 1427 on the font of the Baptistry in
Siena (where Giovanni di Paolo worked). This
relief was by the Florentine sculptor, Ghiberti;
and it was in Florence in the fifteenth century,
more than in Siena or any other centre, that
artists developed an understanding of perspective. The Sienese Giovanni di Paolo shows
St John setting off into a landscape that is
fantastically unreal; but under the influence of
the Florentines, the architectural elements of
the picture are portrayed in a manner that is
more realistic.

The Baptism of Christ by
Lorenzo Ghiberti (1378–1455)
Detail from the Font of the
Baptistry at Siena

Paolo Uccello *St George and the Dragon* (detail). See page 30

PAOLO UCCELLO (*c.* 1397–1475)
St George and the Dragon
56.5 × 74.3 cm

The subject, which is a popular one in art, is derived from *The Golden Legend*. A dragon would stay outside a city only if it was regularly allowed to eat some of the inhabitants. The turn eventually came for the king's daughter to be eaten, but St George arrived in time to wound the dragon, whereupon the princess led the beast back to the city by her girdle. The compiler of the National Gallery catalogue notes that in Uccello's painting the Princess 'by some whim or carelessness continues to wear a girdle'! From the evidence of the Princess's costume the picture may be dated to about 1460. As a painting on canvas it is exceptionally rare; at that time most Italian pictures were painted on wooden panels.

See colour plate page 29

PAOLO UCCELLO (*c.* 1397–1475)
The Rout of San Romano
181 × 320 cm

The Battle of San Romano was fought in June 1432 between the Florentines and the Sienese. Niccolò da Tolentino, the recently appointed Florentine commander, surprised the enemy (and himself) when he came upon them at San Romano in the valley of the River Arno. While awaiting reinforcements (in the background of Uccello's painting foot-soldiers are shown arriving) Niccolò valiantly held out against the Sienese and eventually won the day. The picture is one of three painted by the artist as decoration for a room in the newly built palace of the Medici family in Florence, probably in the 1450s. Originally all three paintings would have formed a frieze well above eye-level about a room.

The picture is not a topographically accurate account of the battle. It is more a commemoration of Niccolò as military leader. On his white horse, he stands out in the picture like a painted equestrian statue. Although he wears a coat of mail, his head is unprotected by armour (a page behind him carries his helmet), and he holds in his right hand the baton of a military commander rather than the sword which he might actually have used in battle. The two parts of the picture, foreground and background, are divided by a rose-hedge. In the foreground the artist is anxious to convey a sense of depth, scale and space, but in the background the soldiers who wander through fields and over hills are depicted with little regard to reality.

Uccello was a Florentine and a pupil of the sculptor Ghiberti. He later worked in Venice as a mosaicist in the basilica of S. Marco. *The Rout of San Romano* contains elements which stem from both Venetian and Florentine traditions. The meticulous painting of the rose-hedge is more Venetian than Florentine; but the experimental attempts at perspective in the foreground of the picture could only have been made in the mid-fifteenth century by an artist who worked in Florence.

PIERO DELLA FRANCESCA (active 1439, d. 1492)
St Michael
133 × 59.4 cm

The picture is probably part of a polyptych completed by 1469 which Piero painted as the high altarpiece of the church of S. Agostino in his home town of San Sepolcro. In the bottom right-hand corner is part of a step which was probably continued, possibly as part of the Virgin's throne, in the (neighbouring) central panel. St Michael's armour is inscribed: *Angelus Potentia dei . . . ha;* but the precise meaning of the inscription is uncertain. *Angelus,* which certainly refers to the Archangel himself, may also be a reference to the donor of the altarpiece: Angelo di Giovanni di Simone d'Angelo.

PIERO DELLA FRANCESCA (active 1439, d. 1492)
The Baptism of Christ
167 × 116 cm

After a period working in Florence, Piero returned to his native San Sepolcro in Umbria soon after 1442 and this picture was one of his first commissions. It was painted as the central panel of a triptych for the high altar of S. Giovanni Battista in San Sepolcro, the town which is depicted in the background of the picture.

The calm dignity of the painting derives in part from Piero's use of extremely delicate colours, and in part from the coherence of the composition. The two-dimensional surface is composed in a pattern of verticals – the tree, the angels, the figure of Christ, etc. – and horizontals – the dove, clouds and left hand of the Baptist. The hovering dove (the Holy Ghost) is at the apex of a triangle of which the Baptist's outstretched arm and leg form one side, and upon further scrutiny this triangle is seen to be almost a pyramid, established by the diminishing scale of the figures: Christ, the neophyte removing his shirt and the figures in the background. Piero is fascinated by the landscape and the reflection of each tree in the river is carefully painted in.

Although now considered one of the greatest painters of the early Italian Renaissance, Piero was for long unappreciated, and it was only in the early 1860s, at about the time this picture was purchased by the National Gallery, that his paintings were becoming generally known.

MASACCIO (1401–1427/9)
The Virgin and Child
135.3 × 73 cm

The picture is reasonably identifiable as the central panel of a polyptych which Masaccio painted for a chapel in the church of the Carmine at Pisa in 1426. The entire altarpiece, which contained many panels, was probably about fifteen feet high. Known as the '*Pisa Polyptych*', it is the only documented work of the artist who is considered, with Giotto a century earlier, one of the founders of Italian Renaissance painting.

Born near Florence, Masaccio probably spent much of his very short working life in that city, although he died in Rome. In the present picture, the musical angels, unrelated in scale to the principal figures of the Virgin and Child, are inserted into the composition to create a decorative effect in a manner which is consistent with the work of Masaccio's lesser Florentine contemporaries. The innovations which Masaccio made, innovations which were to influence all later painters of the Italian Renaissance, are apparent in the seated figure of the Virgin with the Christ Child. They are a 'real' mother and child: the folds of the Virgin's robe fall as they do, not in order to form a decorative surface pattern, but because her body underneath dictates that that is how they should fall. She, as Queen, is seated on a throne, and He sucks grapes: a childish gesture which symbolically suggests His Passion. The fall of light from the left unifies the figures with the space in which they are seated, and throws into relief the solid forms of the Virgin's throne. Painted against a plain gold background, the throne is strongly architectural with carved classical columns, which are carefully painted to be seen, like the altarpiece itself, from below.

This interest in form and in architecture reflects Masaccio's appreciation of the work of his two great Florentine contemporaries: the sculptor Donatello and the architect Brunelleschi.

Ascribed to ANTONIO (*c.* 1432–98) and PIERO
(*c.* 1441–not later than 1496) POLLAIUOLO
The Martyrdom of St Sebastian
291.5 × 202.6 cm

The subject depicted, always called the *Martyrdom of St Sebastian* – although in fact the saint
survived the ordeal – was a popular one in the
Renaissance: it permitted artists commissioned
to paint a religious picture and interested in the
new science of anatomy to portray a nude
figure.

Other preoccupations of the Renaissance
artist were perspective, landscape, the Antique
and the effects of light and shade. The brothers
Antonio and Piero Pollaiuolo, who were

skilled as painters, sculptors, engravers and
goldsmiths, ran a workshop in Florence; and
(according to Vasari) it was for the oratory of
S. Sebastiano, attached to the church of
SS. Annunziata there, that this *Martyrdom of
St Sebastian* was painted in 1475.

The artists' fascination with anatomy is even
more apparent in the figures of the archers than
in that of the nude saint. These six figures
adopt but three different poses which are seen
from different angles; and one sees the same
reversal of viewpoints in the pairs of horses in
the background to right and left. A splendid
ruin is a model of Antique architecture, while
the landscape, an imaginary view of the Arno
valley outside Florence, is painted with a
precision and depth that is breathtaking.

SANDRO BOTTICELLI (*c.* 1445–1510)
Venus and Mars
69.2 × 173.4 cm

The picture shows Venus, Goddess of Love, with Mars, God of War, lying beside her asleep. Like other paintings of the theme, the picture is an allegory of Beauty and Valour, or Strife conquered by Love. Baby satyrs play with the discarded armour of Mars; one of them, possibly at the command of Venus, attempts to awaken him by blowing a conch shell in his ear; another climbs into his armour and clutches a gourd. From their nest in the trunk of the tree wasps swarm about the head of Mars, probably demonstrating that the pleasure of love (as brought by Venus) may also be accompanied by pain. In the distance is the sea from which the goddess was born.

It is not certain when, or for whom, the picture was painted. Among Botticelli's patrons in Florence, were the Vespucci family, whose coat of arms includes *vespae* (wasps), and it would not be unusual in the Renaissance for a painter to play upon such a heraldic allusion. Painted oblong panels like this one (there are others in the National Gallery) were probably incorporated in the wainscoting of a room or perhaps used as bed-heads. Certainly the subject of the present picture, the conquering power of love, would be a suitable one for the decoration of a marriage bed.

Botticelli, now perhaps the most famous of all late fifteenth-century Florentine painters, was only 'rediscovered' in the second half of the nineteenth century; and the National Gallery acquired five of his paintings between 1857 and 1878. The fragile weariness of his Madonnas and his emphasis on line and contour appealed to the aesthetic sensibilities of the late Victorians.

ALESSO BALDOVINETTI (*c.* 1426–99)
Portrait of a Lady in Yellow
62.9 × 40.6 cm

When this Florentine portrait of the second half of the fifteenth century was purchased by the Gallery in 1866 it was thought to have been painted by Piero della Francesca. It was Roger Fry in 1911 who first suggested that it might be by the Florentine Baldovinetti – an attribution which is now fully accepted.

The identity of the sitter remains unknown; but the pattern on her sleeve probably offers some clue. The flowers could for example be part of the lady's coat of arms, for her costume and jewels are so luxurious that she was almost certainly noble.

Profile portraits became popular in the Renaissance, reflecting an interest in the Antique; and this painted image of a lady is reminiscent of the profile heads to be seen on Antique gems and coins.

PIERO DI COSIMO (*c.* 1462–after 1515)
A Mythological Subject
65.4 × 184.2 cm

The subject of the picture remains unidentified, but it is probably taken from some Renaissance poem rather than from classical mythology, though in the past it has been thought that the picture represented some incident from the story of Cephalus and Procris. A nymph with a wound in her neck lies partly naked on the ground while a satyr (and a faithful dog)

grieves over her. In the background is a river or lake with several birds and animals.

Vasari wrote that Piero di Cosimo 'had by nature a most lofty spirit, and he was very strange and different in fancy from other youths . . . he set himself often to observe such animals, plants, or other things as Nature at times creates out of caprice, or by chance; in which he found a pleasure and satisfaction that drove him quite out of his mind with delight; and he spoke of them so often in his discourse, that at times, although he found pleasure in them, it became wearisome to others'.

SANDRO BOTTICELLI (*c.* 1445–1510)
Portrait of a young Man
37.5 × 28.3 cm

In the nineteenth century this portrait was thought to be by the early fifteenth-century Florentine artist, Masaccio (1401–27/29), and it was as such that it was purchased by the National Gallery in 1859. Now, however, it is accepted as by Botticelli, one of the most individual artists working in late fifteenth-century Florence. In 1481/2 he was in Rome, painting frescoes in the Sistine Chapel, and it was probably shortly after his return to

Florence that this portrait was painted. The sitter has not been identified.

Botticelli originally trained as a goldsmith and subsequently learned painting, probably from Filippo Lippi. In his early years he painted both pagan and religious subjects as well as portraits and was eventually successful enough to run a studio. From about 1490, however, like many of his Florentine contemporaries, he was influenced by the preaching of the Dominican monk, Savonarola (who was burned in Florence in 1498); his subject-matter became more religious and his style less naturalistic than in his earlier work, e.g. the late *Mystic Nativity* in the National Gallery.

COSIMO TURA (before 1431–95)
The Virgin and Child enthroned
239.4 × 101.6 cm

The picture is the central panel of an altarpiece from the church of S. Giorgio fuori le Mura at Ferrara. Cosimo Tura worked in Ferrara from 1451, mainly at the court of the Este family. The throne on which the Virgin is seated is inscribed with extracts in Hebrew from the Ten Commandments, while above, also on the throne, are the symbols of the four Evangelists. On the throne, therefore, the Old Testament is juxtaposed with the New, for it was by the life of Christ, as recorded by the Evangelists in the New Testament, that the prophecies of the Old Testament were fulfilled.

The altarpiece, of which this is part, belonged to the Roverella family, and the Latin inscription on the organ case (now only decipherable in part) suggests that it was installed on the death of a member of the family. The inscription (recorded in a book of 1492) reads: *Arise Child. The Roverella family strikes at the gate. Grant that the way be opened. The law says 'Knock, and thou shalt be within'.*

Cosimo Tura was the first great Ferrarese painter and had a highly distinctive decorative style. He was influenced by Mantegna, who worked in neighbouring Mantua, while his colouring owes much to Piero della Francesca, who had earlier painted a cycle of frescoes (now lost) at Ferrara.

SASSETTA (1392?–1450)
St Francis decides to become a Soldier
87 × 52.4 cm

The picture, which is one of a series of seven panels in the Gallery, is part of a large altarpiece which Sassetta painted between 1437 and 1444 for the high altar of the church of S. Francesco at San Sepolcro. The altarpiece had a large central picture (now in the Berenson collection, Florence) of *St Francis Triumphant,* and smaller pictures (such as the National Gallery panels) depicted scenes from his life. There are two incidents shown in the colour plate. Intending to go to war, St Francis prepared rich clothes, but in an act of generosity gave them away to a knight poorer than himself. Later while he slept an angel showed

St Francis renounces his earthly father

him in a dream a palace decorated with military flags and floating in the air. At first St Francis interpreted the dream as meaning that he should follow a military career, but as the banners were those of Christ, he later realized that his life should be spent in the service of God.

Sassetta and Giovanni di Paolo are the two greatest of Sienese fifteenth-century painters. In Siena, Byzantine traditions in painting lingered longer than in Florence, and so Sassetta's pictures are less 'realistic' than those of contemporary Florentine painters. He paints the popular legend of St Francis as taking place in a delightful toyland setting, and he uses colour in an enchanting manner. The architecture used throughout to enhance the narrative of the scenes is painted most meticulously; but these palaces and churches are flimsy stage sets whose floors have never been trodden, and whose doors have never been closed.

Other panels from the altarpiece, which may have remained in the church until the eighteenth century, are now at Chantilly and in the Louvre.

The Pope accords recognition to the Franciscan Order

St Francis bears witness to the Christian faith before the Sultan

Andrea Mantegna (*c.* 1430–1506)
The Agony in the Garden
62.9 × 80 cm

The subject is taken from the Gospels. After
the Last Supper, Christ, knowing that He had
been betrayed by Judas, went with three of His
disciples to the Garden of Gethsemane. Asking
them to keep watch, He went and prayed, only
to discover on His return that they had fallen
asleep. In Mantegna's picture, *putti,* bearing
the instruments of the Passion – column, cross,
sponge and spear – appear to the kneeling
Christ, while Judas leads a group of soldiers
from walled Jerusalem in the background. In
the foreground are the sleeping disciples,
Peter, James and John.

Mantegna's picture, which may have been
painted some time in the 1460s, probably
influenced Giovanni Bellini's treatment of the
same theme, also in the National Gallery. The
two men were brothers-in-law, as Mantegna
married the sister of Giovanni and Gentile
Bellini in 1453. Both Bellini brothers were
influenced by Mantegna, who from 1459/60
worked at Mantua in the service of the
Gonzaga family.

Some of Mantegna's paintings are executed
in a grisaille technique in imitation of sculpture, and there are examples of these in the
National Gallery. They were probably painted
under the influence of the Florentine sculptor,
Donatello, whose work at Padua Mantegna
could have seen when he was a young man.

CARLO CRIVELLI (active 1457–93)
*The Virgin and Child with St Jerome and
St Sebastian* (The '*Madonna della Rondine*')
Main panel: 150 × 107 cm
Signed: CAROLVS · CRIVELLVS ·
VENETVS · MILES · PINXIT

The painting, which derives its name from the
swallow (*rondine*) perched on the Virgin's
throne, is an altarpiece complete in its original
frame and it comes originally from the church
of S. Francesco at Matelica. The arms on the
step in front of the Virgin's throne are those of
the Ottoni, the ruling family of Matelica. The
saints are (left) St Jerome, depicted as a Doctor
of the Church in cardinal's robes and holding a
book and a model of a church, and (right)
St Sebastian, shown (unusually) fully dressed
and elegantly holding an arrow.

Like all Crivelli's paintings, the picture is
immensely decorative. The garlands of fruit,
flowers and vegetables which adorn the

Virgin's throne, however, have a symbolic as
well as an ornamental function. The swallow
and gourd are symbols of resurrection, and the
apple – the fruit of the Fall – held in Christ's
hand is a symbol of salvation.

Crivelli was a Venetian (he signs himself as
such throughout his life) who during his
twenties was imprisoned in Venice for the
abduction of a sailor's wife. After his release,
about the mid-1460s, he seems to have left
Venice and spent the rest of his life in that
region of Italy around Urbino known as the
Marches. (In 1490 he was knighted by Ferdinand II of Naples and thereafter signed
himself, as here, '*miles*'.) He worked in relative
isolation, and his style remained highly individual, although the garlands of fruit and
flowers in his pictures remind one of his
Paduan contemporary, Mantegna; and his
brilliantly decorative stuffs and costumes
suggest an International Gothic style as seen in
the work of the Veronese painter, Pisanello.

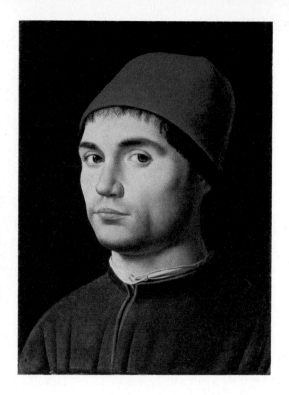

x-ray photograph

ANTONELLO DA MESSINA
(active 1456, d. 1479)
Portrait of a Man
35.6 × 25.4 cm

The picture is judged on stylistic grounds to
have been painted about 1475–9. The bottom
has been sawn off, but presumably, as in other
portraits by Antonello, it showed a ledge
bearing a *cartellino* with the artist's signature.
An inscription (which may date from the
seventeenth century) on the back suggests that
it is a self-portrait. If so, it would seem that
Antonello (whose date of birth is unknown)
was still a relatively young man when he died.
The stare of the sitter towards the spectator is
consistent with self-portraiture, when artists
have to paint from mirror images of themselves; but other portraits by Antonello of
different sitters have the eyes treated in the
same manner. X-rays reveal that the position of
the eyes has been altered and that originally

they looked in the opposite direction; but an
artist such as Antonello, fascinated by optical
effect, might well have used two mirrors when
painting his own portrait.

For a painting of its age the picture is in very
good condition. The portrait has a reality
which is almost frightening, with light falling
on the face creating shadows and throwing the
head into relief against the plain black background. Details such as the lips, the shadow of
a beard, the folds in the sitter's white collar and
the individually painted hairs on his forehead
are minutely observed. This is consistent with
the style of artists who learned much from
contemporary Netherlandish painting, which
also contained much closely observed detail.
Antonello probably never visited the Netherlands, but at Naples, where he worked for
some years before 1456, there were paintings
by Jan van Eyck and Rogier van der Weyden,
the two greatest fifteenth-century Netherlandish painters.

45

G.B. Cima da Conegliano (?1459/60–1517/18)
David and Jonathan
40.6 × 39.4 cm

David, by killing the Philistine Goliath, had delivered the Israelites from the Philistines. The youthful hero's triumphal entry into Jerusalem bearing the head of Goliath is the episode most usually depicted in painting, and this subject was regarded as an Old Testament prefiguration of Christ's own triumphal entry into Jerusalem. Cima's picture is more unusual, if not unique, in showing David accompanied by Jonathan. It was on the day of his triumph, and before he went to Jerusalem, that David made his pact of friendship with the beloved son of King Saul, Jonathan: 'The soul of Jonathan was kindled in the soul of David, and Jonathan loved him as his own soul.' Nothing is known of the origin of the picture, but it is possible that it was commissioned from Cima in commemoration of a particular friendship.

Cima was a contemporary in Venice of Giovanni Bellini by whom he was much influenced. The beautiful landscape in the present picture compares well with those in the paintings of Bellini, landscapes which were inspired by the Veneto, the countryside neighbouring Venice: the walled town (supposedly Jerusalem) in the background of *David and Jonathan* is bathed in a north Italian light.

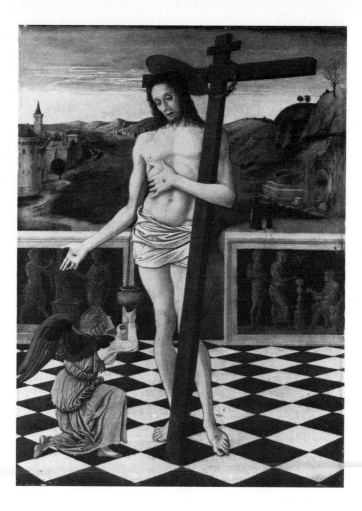

GIOVANNI BELLINI (active *c.* 1459, d. 1516)
The Blood of the Redeemer
47 × 34.3 cm

The subject of the picture, which is a mystical one rather than representing a particular incident, is self-explanatory: Christ's blood shed as His sacrifice to save sinners. Christ stands on a tiled floor holding the Cross which bears the Crown of Thorns. A parapet behind Him is decorated with classical reliefs showing scenes of sacrifice. Their position, and the fact that, in spite of every effort to identify them, they seem not to represent any particular subjects of pagan sacrifice, suggest that al-though they allude to the subject-matter of the picture they are of secondary importance: indeed Christ's right hand obscures part of one relief. The background landscape too relates to Bellini's subject-matter: on the right the land is barren with the ruined remains of an Antique pagan column and gateway. Two figures, turning their back on this landscape, look towards a town on the side of a verdant valley. Here is life, the life for which Christ's sacrifice was made, and this is the new Jerusalem.

On stylistic grounds the picture seems to have been painted about 1465, and is there-fore about contemporary with the *Agony in the Garden* by Giovanni Bellini, also in the National Gallery.

GIOVANNI BELLINI (active *c.* 1459, d. 1516)
The Doge Leonardo Loredan
61.6 × 45.1 cm
Signed: IOANNES BELLINVS

Leonardo Loredan was born in 1436 and was elected Doge of Venice in 1501. In Bellini's portrait he wears the Doge's cap, or *corno*, and sumptuous robes of state. The style of the painting indicates that the portrait was painted sometime early in the sixteenth century, and it seems most likely that it was painted on Loredan's election as Doge. He would then have been aged sixty-five.

The Doge was the elected head of the Venetian republican government, but such was the political organization of the state that his actual powers were almost nil. He was merely a figurehead, a symbol of the continuance of the Venetian Republic, and almost imprisoned by his office.

This impassive portrait of Doge Loredan is conceived as the image of a ruler. The form is that of a sculpted bust and neither hands nor background are shown. Nothing distracts from the head of the grave old man. Yet the picture, perhaps the most famous of all Venetian portraits, conveys almost miraculously the flesh and blood of the sitter. This is a tribute to the painter, Giovanni Bellini, the first truly great Venetian artist.

PISANELLO (living *c.* 1395, d. ?1455)
The Virgin and Child with St George and St Anthony Abbot
47 × 29.2 cm
Signed: *pisanus/pi*

The two saints are St Anthony Abbot (accompanied by a hog and carrying a bell) and St George (accompanied by a dragon and wearing a fantastically decorative costume). The Virgin and Child 'clothed in the sun' may be a reference to the Woman and Child in Revelation xii. The artist's signature in the foreground seems almost disguised as part of the fauna.

The immense popularity of the picture in the National Gallery probably owes much to the appeal of the sumptuously extravagant figure of St George. He is an elegant fifteenth-century courtier and his costume is most likely inspired by those of the members of the Este court at Ferrara where Pisanello was employed. Many drawings by Pisanello survive, among them sketches of costumes similar to that of St George.

Bust of *A Member of the Capponi Family* by an unidentified Florentine sculptor of the fifteenth century. (Victoria and Albert Museum)

48

IOANNES BELLINVS

Detail of view from the window

ROBERT CAMPIN (1378/9–1444)
The Virgin and Child before a Firescreen
63.5 × 49.5 cm

The Virgin, seated (presumably on a low footstool) before a bench, and leaning on a cupboard, is feeding the Christ Child. To the right a strip has been added to the panel and the cupboard and chalice are modern. The background detail and the violently receding tiled floor have the effect of making the Virgin seem unduly large.

Apart from the chalice, symbol of Christ's Passion, the picture could be a simple domestic interior with a mother nursing her child in front of an open window. However, much of the domestic detail has a religious significance. The firescreen, which shields the Virgin from the flames of the fire, serves also as a natural halo. The lions decorating the wooden bench remind one of the throne of Solomon which

was similarly decorated, and upon which Solomon placed his mother, Bathsheba, thereby providing an Old Testament parallel to the Coronation of the Virgin. The Virgin is seated, not upon the bench, but almost on the floor, and in that she approximates to a common fifteenth-century type: the Madonna of Humility. It was out of humility that all Christian virtues grew, just as the Christ Child grew when nurtured by the Virgin.

Robert Campin worked at Tournai from the early years of the fifteenth century. He may have been one and the same as 'the Master of Flémalle' mentioned in the documents, and Rogier van der Weyden may have been his pupil. His work was of enormous importance, for like his great contemporary, Jan van Eyck, he brought a new realism to Netherlandish painting in the fifteenth century, a realism of a type demonstrated by this rather plump Flemish girl who provided the model for the Madonna in an upstairs room in Tournai.

JAN VAN EYCK (active 1422, d. 1441)
A Man in a Turban
33.3 × 25.8 cm

The portrait is in its original frame which, as in the case of other paintings by Van Eyck, is inscribed at the top: 'Als ich can' in semi-Greek lettering. These are thought to be the first words of the Flemish proverb 'As I can, but not as I would', and, in the context, they presumably mean that the painter has done his best in portraying the likeness of the sitter.

The man, who wears a fashionable contemporary head-dress of red material, is thought by some to be Van Eyck himself. The basis for such an hypothesis is his engaging glance, with eyes turned directly towards the spectator, as though they had been painted from a mirror.

Page 52

JAN VAN EYCK (active 1422, d. 1441)
'The Arnolfini Marriage' (*The Marriage of Giovanni Arnolfini and Giovanna Cenami*)
81.8 × 59.7 cm
Signed: *Johannes de eyck*
          fuit hic. 1434

The man is Giovanni di Arrigo Arnolfini, a merchant from Lucca who lived a great deal at Bruges and was buried there in 1472. The lady is Giovanna Cenami, the daughter of another Lucchese merchant who lived at Paris. The picture would have been painted at Bruges where Van Eyck, who played an important part in the discovery of oil-painting technique, was working in the service of the Duke of Burgundy from 1425. The picture is a marriage portrait, and would seem to show the marriage actually taking place. The signature, 'Jan van Eyck was here', suggests the painter's presence as a witness. At that time a couple might contract a marriage without the services of a priest simply by mutual consent with appropriate words and actions. Here the couple hold hands, and he gestures as if taking an oath, while the position of Madame Arnolfini's left hand may well symbolize marriage. The single candle in the chandelier is a marriage candle and the griffon terrier is a symbol of fidelity.

Within the relative gloom of this room, therefore, the couple make their solemn oath, while outside in the garden, the sun shines and the trees bear fruit. Van Eyck miraculously reflects the scene in the mirror (decorated with scenes from Christ's Passion) on the back wall, and in that mirror two people are reflected as they enter the room: one of these may be the painter himself, but he does not intrude upon the calm dignity of the couple, and only the dog registers his presence. This detail is perhaps the key to the picture's charm: a symbolic act is almost disguised by the realism of the domestic detail.

Detail of the mirror

JAN VAN EYCK '*The Arnolfini Marriage*'. See page 51

Master of the Life of the Virgin
(active second half 15th century)
The Conversion of St Hubert
123.8 × 83.2 cm

According to legend, as a young man St Hubert was given to worldly pleasures, in particular the chase. While hunting one Good Friday he was confronted by a stag bearing a crucifix between its antlers, and was thereupon converted to Christianity. His legend is sometimes confused with that of St Eustace who was similarly converted, but Eustace was a Roman soldier of the second century, while Hubert (*c.* 656–727) became first Bishop of Liège. In the present picture scenes of hunting and hawking are shown in the background, while in the foreground St Hubert kneels before the stag.

The picture is part of an altarpiece (probably a diptych) which seems to have been painted some time in the 1490s for the Benedictine abbey church at Werden near Düsseldorf. The church was renovated and new altarpieces installed by the Abbot Grimholt, who ruled between 1484 and 1517. In 1803 the abbey was suppressed and the pictures from it were taken over by the Prussian authorities and subsequently sold. *The Conversion of St Hubert*, which is one of four panels from the altarpiece, later formed part of the German Krüger collection, purchased by the National Gallery in 1854. The whole altarpiece has recently been reassembled so that (as originally) *The Conversion of St Hubert* is on the left inside panel with *The Mass of St Hubert* opposite; two groups of saints form the outside.

The name of the painter is unknown, but he is given the title used by the Gallery because of a series of eight panels by him depicting scenes from the life of the Virgin. One of these panels is now in the National Gallery; the remainder are at Munich. Whoever he may have been, he worked at Cologne during the second half of the fifteenth century, although his style, which betrays the influence of the Netherlandish painters Dieric Bouts and Rogier van der Weyden, suggests that he may have trained in the Netherlands. He also seems to have employed a workshop; *The Conversion of St Hubert* (which is of exceptionally high quality) and *The Mass* are both notably superior in quality to the outsides of the altarpiece, suggesting that the most important paintings were painted by the Master himself and the remainder by his workshop.

St Joseph by Rogier van der Weyden (Gulbenkian Foundation, Lisbon) shown in association with part of the National Gallery's *Magdalen reading*

ROGIER VAN DER WEYDEN (*c.* 1399–1464)
The Magdalen reading
61.6 × 54.6 cm

This picture is a fragment from the right-hand side of a much larger picture, other parts of which survive in the Gulbenkian collection, Lisbon. The original picture, which is in part recorded by a late fifteenth-century drawing after it, showed the Virgin and Child with Saints John the Baptist, John the Evangelist, Joseph, Mary Magdalen, and probably one other saint. The National Gallery fragment is that part which represents the Magdalen (recognizable by the jar of ointment which she used to anoint Christ's feet). Parts of two other figures, to the left and above her, are also visible: that holding a rosary is probably St Joseph – his head is one of the Lisbon fragments – and the kneeling figure to the left (his toes just visible) can be identified as St John the Evangelist. The background was, until recently, overpainted in black. The picture was purchased by the National Gallery in 1860.

The Magdalen, absorbed in her reading, has a quiet piety. This is uncharacteristic of the painter, whose work is generally more 'emotional' than that of the other great Netherlandish painter of the fifteenth century, Jan van Eyck. The cut-off view through the window is of a canal with a shooting archer on its bank, and a figure walking on the opposite bank is reflected in the water. Like other contemporary Netherlandish painters, Rogier is fascinated by the depiction of minute details such as the nails on the floor. The effects of falling light are also explored: St Joseph's beads have bright highlights while the clasps on the book and the wooden tracery of the cupboard are delineated by areas of light and shade.

Rogier, who lived at Tournai, was the most important painter working in Flanders in the mid-fifteenth century. He was probably the same person as Rogelet de la Pasture who was apprenticed at Tournai to Robert Campin between 1427 and 1432.

HANS MEMLINC (active 1465, d. 1494)
Triptych: *The Virgin and Child with Saints and Donors* ('*The Donne Triptych*')
Central part: 70.8 × 70.5 cm,
wings: 71 × 30.5 cm

The Virgin is enthroned with the Christ Child on her lap. He blesses Sir John Donne (the donor of the altarpiece), who is protected by St Catherine, while his wife, kneeling on the opposite side with their daughter, is protected by St Barbara. Sir John Donne, who was knighted at Tewkesbury in 1471, died in 1503. He was a supporter of the Yorkist cause and in the picture both he and his wife wear Yorkist collars of roses and suns with Edward IV's pendant, the Lion of March. The scene is shown taking place within an architectural setting which is continuous throughout the three parts of the Triptych; the arms of the donor decorate the capitals and the glass of the window. On the left wing is St John the Baptist, on the right St John the Evangelist.

Light floods in from the outside, making a contrast between the interior scene and the exterior landscape. As in other early Netherlandish paintings, the Virgin and Saints are conceived as belonging to a heavenly world, while the landscape is an earthly one. The two worlds are connected by the figure who peeps in through the window in the left wing and it is possible that this is a self-portrait of the artist.

Sir John Donne is known to have visited Bruges (where Memlinc worked) in 1468 and again in 1477; but as he lived much at Calais he might easily have visited the painter at any time. Stylistically the Triptych would seem to have been painted some time late in the 1470s; it descended in the family of Sir John Donne until 1957, when it was acquired by the National Gallery. Memlinc was probably a pupil of Rogier van der Weyden by whom, as well as Dieric Bouts, he was influenced. His pictures have a tranquil, pious quality and are painted in very beautiful colours.

JAN GOSSAERT called *Mabuse*
(active 1503, d. 1532)
A Little Girl, (Jacqueline de Bourgogne?)
38 × 28.9 cm

The girl is traditionally identified as Jacqueline de Bourgogne, daughter of Adolphe de Bourgogne (a patron of Gossaert) and Anne de Bergues, whom Gossaert is known to have painted. Jacqueline de Bourgogne's date of birth is unknown, but her parents were married in 1509, and as this portrait may be dated about 1520 on the basis of costume, she may have been about nine or ten at the time.

Her costume, which is elaborately embroidered with pearls, is very sumptuous and expensive. In her left hand she holds an

armillary sphere—a skeleton celestial globe of metal rings representing the equator, the tropics, etc. By pointing to the sphere, she would seem to be indicating something to the spectator; perhaps her age, or even her destiny. The sphere is inscribed with letters, but they are upside down, so this exquisite astronomical instrument is nothing but a toy to this enchanting little girl. Her presence is made all the more real to us by the fact that she is painted in front of a simulated picture frame.

Gossaert, who is called Mabuse because his parents came from Maubeuge in Hainault, worked in Antwerp in his early years. About 1508/9 he travelled to Italy and on his return worked chiefly at Middelburg, where Adolphe de Bourgogne lived. The painter's early style was derived from Hugo van der Goes and influenced by Dürer, but after his trip to Italy his work became more Italianate.

background, but a figure seated in a three-dimensional space – a space filled with air. The light side of the man's face is thrown into relief by the dark background of the shutter, and the dark side of his face by the light wall.

Bouts was particularly influenced by Rogier van der Weyden – here the pose of the sitter reflects Rogier's work. Jan van Eyck was also an influence, for Bouts paid great attention to the effects of illumination. But Bouts was an innovator as a landscape painter, and in this portrait the view through the window contains, in a tiny space, an immense landscape with a closely observed brownish-green foreground giving way to distant blue hills.

Pieter Bruegel the Elder
(active 1551, d. 1569)
The Adoration of the Kings
111 × 83.2 cm
Signed: *Brvegel M.D. LXIIII*

Pieter Bruegel was influenced by Hieronymus Bosch and in turn influenced his son, the landscape and flower painter and collaborator of Rubens, Jan Bruegel the Elder called 'Velvet' Bruegel. *The Adoration of the Kings* is interesting in this context as it relates to two other pictures, by Bosch and Velvet Bruegel, in the National Gallery. One of the background figures wears a hat with an arrow through it as does one of Christ's tormentors in *Christ Mocked* by Bosch (page 174); while the poses of the Moorish king, St Joseph and his companion and the soldier are repeated in Velvet Bruegel's *Adoration* painted thirty-four years later. Pieter Bruegel the Elder is perhaps best known for his series of paintings representing the seasons of the year.

Dieric Bouts (living *c.* 1448, d. 1475)
Portrait of a Man
31.8 × 20.3 cm
Dated: . *1462*

The picture, prominently dated 1462, is in excellent condition and is the earliest dated work of the artist, who worked at Louvain. It is thought also to be the earliest example of a type of portrait design – a figure in a room with a view out of a window – which became a commonplace in late fifteenth-century Netherlandish painting. Such portraits (although probably not in the case of the present picture) often formed one half of a diptych with a representation of the Virgin and Child on the opposite wing. In such cases the view of the landscape suggested the earthly habitation of the sitter in contrast to the heavenly one of the Virgin.

Here the sitter seems lost in thought, the position of his hands and eyes suggesting that he is at prayer. Without showing the ceiling, Bouts defines the corner of the room by the subtle fall of shadows on the wall behind. The portrait therefore is not just a head against a

MARINUS VAN REYMERSWAELE
(active ?1509, d. after ?1567)
The Two Tax-gatherers
92.1 × 74.3 cm

The Dutch writing in the book may be deciphered, and from it it is clear that the man on the left is composing an account of municipal revenues from imposts on wine, beer, fish, etc. As mention is made of a 'visbrugge', i.e. a fish-market on a bridge, it is possible that the municipality concerned is Reymerswaele, one of the few towns where such a thing existed. Indeed, in the document above the head of the man on the right Reymerswaele is actually referred to as well as Cornelis Danielsz, the name of a man who was living there in 1524.

However, rather than being an actual portrait (the figures are dressed in fantastic costumes), the picture is more probably intended as a satire on the iniquities of extortion and usury. It is one of a group of pictures of similar subjects by Marinus. Some of the coins in the picture have been identified, and they preclude a date of execution before 1526.

JOACHIM PATENIER (active 1515, d. not later than 1524)
St Jerome in a rocky Landscape
36.2 × 34.3 cm

Several incidents from the legend of St Jerome are shown taking place in this weird and beautiful early sixteenth-century landscape. In the foreground, before a cavernous rock, the ascetic saint removes the thorn from the paw of the lion which later became his friend. Behind, and to the left, a blind man is led across a foot-bridge by a dog, alluding to the fact that St Jerome was the patron saint of those suffering from diseases of the eyes. In the centre of the picture, in the forecourt of a monastery an abbot receives two merchants with camels and an ass. It was the task of St Jerome's lion to guard the ass of the monastery, but one day it was stolen by two merchants with camels. Later the lion, recognizing the ass, brought it to the monastery with the merchants, who thereupon asked pardon of the abbot. To the left is a pagan altar with an outdoor idol and above it a castle.

The landscape, both in its treatment and use of subject-matter, a penitent saint in the wilderness (a theme which Patenier frequently painted), is characteristic of the artist. Dürer (who met Patenier in Antwerp in 1520/21) referred to him as 'a good landscape painter', and indeed he may be thought of as one of the first landscape painters; before him landscape in northern art was limited to the backgrounds of other types of painting. Patenier's paintings were very popular with contemporary collectors; he employed a workshop, and had many imitators.

He was born near Namur on the River Meuse in Belgium; and it was the natural rock formation of the river valley near his birthplace which inspired his view of landscape. He later worked at Antwerp where he died young some time before 1524. Antwerp was then a trading port which attracted rich merchants from most parts of Europe, many of whom collected pictures. Patenier's small and portable landscapes appealed to them; perhaps also they saw themselves as the penitent merchants whom Patenier included in several of the pictures which he painted on the theme of St Jerome.

LUCAS CRANACH THE ELDER (1472–1553)
Cupid complaining to Venus
81.3 × 54.6 cm
Signed with Cranach's device of a winged
dragon

The subject of the picture is derived from a
third-century BC Greek poem by Theocritus,
Idyll XIX, The Honeycomb Stealer. The poem,
lines from which Cranach has inscribed in
Latin on the painting, tells how Cupid com-
plained to Venus of being stung by bees while
stealing honeycombs: 'While the boy Cupid
plunders honey from the beehive, the bee
fastens on his finger with piercing sting.'
Cranach, however, adds a further couplet to
the inscription, not found in Theocritus, that
reads, 'So in like manner the brief and fleeting
pleasure which we seek injures us with sad
pain.' Latin translations of Theocritus' poem,
published in Germany in the 1520s, probably
inspired Cranach; while the several versions of
the subject by him (there are others in the
Borghese Gallery, Rome, the Berlin Museum
and elsewhere) suggest that the moral content
of the theme must have appealed to Renaissance patrons.

Cranach, who was also an etcher and
designer of woodcuts, was a great portraitist
and is thought to have painted the first
independent full-length portraits. He spent
much of his life as Court Painter to the Electors
of Saxony at Wittenberg, and in the refined and
sophisticated circles of the court he found
patrons for those erotic female nudes upon
which his fame perhaps rests. Sometimes these
represent *Eve*, sometimes *Charity*, sometimes
The Three Graces or, as in the case of the present
picture, *Venus*. Here she coyly raises her leg as
she glances at the spectator; and the fact that
she is not entirely nude, but wears a sumptuously fashionable hat and necklace, only
emphasizes her eroticism still further. She is a
'contemporary' girl, but the picture dem-
onstrates that the pleasures of love which this
'contemporary' Venus can bring to the courtiers of Wittenberg may also be accompanied by
pain. In the forest background a stag and doe
grazing together allude further to the subject-
matter of the painting, while to the right a
disconcertingly real-looking German landscape makes the girl's pretence of being the
Antique goddess *Venus* seem all the more
unconvincing.

HANS HOLBEIN THE YOUNGER (1497/8–1543)
Christina of Denmark, Duchess of Milan
179.1 × 82.6 cm

She was the younger daughter of Christian II
of Denmark and was born in 1522. At the age
of eleven she was married by proxy to Francesco Maria Sforza, Duke of Milan, who died
two years later. This portrait, in which she
wears mourning, is probably derived from a
drawing made by Holbein on 12 March 1538
when she sat to him for 'thre owers space' at
Brussels. Holbein was employed as Court
Painter by Henry VIII, and the portrait of
Christina was painted at a time when Henry
had plans to marry her. Christina, however,
never became England's Queen, and in fact
only visited the country twice (after Henry's
death, one might add!). Nevertheless,
Holbein's startlingly simple image of her as a
sixteen-year-old girl is better known and loved
than most portraits of English royalty.

HANS HOLBEIN THE YOUNGER (1497/8–1543)
Jean de Dinteville and Georges de Selve
('*The Ambassadors*')
207 × 209 cm
Inscribed: IOANNES/HOLBEIN PINGEBAT/1533

The sitters are Jean de Dinteville (1504–55), Seigneur de Polisy, Bailly de Troyes, who was French ambassador to England during 1533, and his friend Georges de Selve (1508/9–41), Bishop of Lavaur, who visited him in London in April/May 1533. The mosaic floor is derived from that still existing in Westminster Abbey. The objects on the what-not are (lower shelf) a lute with a broken string, a case of lutes, an open hymnbook with music, a half-open book

of arithmetic, a terrestrial globe and (top shelf) various astronomical instruments including a cylindrical sundial, which gives the date as 11 April, and a polyhedral sundial, which gives the time as 10.30 a.m. The ages of both sitters are given in the portrait: that of Dinteville on the sheath of his dagger, De Selve's on the book under his elbow. A crucifix is partly visible in the top left-hand corner, the brooch on Dinteville's cap is ornamented with a skull, and, most striking of all, the curious shape across the foreground of the picture also assumes the form of a skull when viewed from the extreme right.

Various attempts have been made at explaining the meaning of the picture. The elaborate

still-life would seem to demonstrate that the sitters were rich, powerful, learned and accomplished. But the presence of the skulls would suggest that this still-life is also a *vanitas*: that is, one which serves to indicate the transcience of human existence. The skulls and broken lutestring are reminders of death, the various timepieces indicative of the march of time.

The theme of mortality was one which interested Holbein. In some of his early work, and in a portrait such as *The Ambassadors*, the theme is all the more tellingly illustrated because of the realism of the details.

HANS BALDUNG GRIEN (1484/5–1545)
Portrait of a Man
59.3 × 48.9 cm
Dated: 1514

The identity of the sitter in this portrait, which was painted in 1514, remains unknown. It seems unlikely that he is, as has been suggested, one of the Margraves of Baden for whom Baldung worked from about 1510. The man is, however, a nobleman, as one of the badges which he wears on a chain about his neck is part of the insignia of the Order of Our Lady of the Swan, and shows the Virgin holding the Child in a crescent moon with rays. The other badge, a fish and a falcon on a branch, indicates that he was a member of the Swabian Fish and Falcon jousting company.

The portrait was once believed to be by Dürer, who may have been Baldung's teacher and whose style sometimes resembles his.

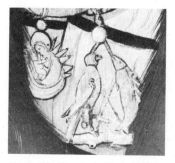

Detail of the *Portrait of a Man* by Baldung showing the badges worn by the sitter

Ascribed to DÜRER (1471–1528)
The Painter's Father
51 × 40.3 cm
Inscribed: *1479 . Albrecht . Thvrer . der . elter . vnd . alt . 70 ior*

This picture is probably the one described in 1639 as follows: '(the painters father) in a black antique old Hungarian fashioned black cap, in a dark yellow green robe, where his hands are hidden in the wide sleeves, painted upon a reddish all cracked board'.

That picture was presented in 1636 to Charles I by the city of Nuremberg, Dürer's place of birth, together with a self-portrait of the artist, now in the Prado, Madrid. In spite of this reliable pedigree, the portrait has been the subject of controversy. While it is accepted as probably the oldest and best of several extant versions of the design, not all scholars are agreed that it is by Dürer himself. The citizens of Nuremberg in 1636 almost certainly thought that it was, and so did Charles I; but the drawing of all but the head in the picture is not of a quality that might be expected from the greatest artist of the Northern Renaissance.

Albrecht Dürer the Elder, who would have been seventy when this image of him was recorded, was a goldsmith working in Nuremberg and was also his son's first teacher.

Lucas van Leyden (active 1508, d. 1533)
A Man aged 38
47.6 × 40.6 cm

Portraits by Lucas, who was primarily an engraver but also a designer of stained glass, are relatively rare. At Leyden he was a pupil of his father (by whom no works are known), but in 1521 he visited Antwerp and there met Dürer. It may have been at this time that the present picture was executed, as it belongs to a type which probably reflects the influence of Dürer.

The brilliant deployment of line characteristic of a great engraver is apparent in the portrait. The tightly closed lips are almost incised and the brightly lit right cheek forms a contour against the black of his cap; but most of all perhaps it is in the black and blue mantle that line is most subtly and beautifully used. His age, thirty-eight, is inscribed on the piece of paper which he clutches in his hand.

By tradition Lucas (whose exact date of birth is unknown) is regarded, on account of some highly competent engravings which might have been executed while he was still a boy, as having been a child prodigy. A study of a series of self-portraits by him would also indicate that he might have been of a delicate, even neurotic, temperament; his earliest biographer, Van Mander, said that he led a dilettante life, worked in bed and dressed in yellow silk clothes; but he might have been confusing him with another artist.

LEONARDO DA VINCI (1452–1519)
'*The Virgin of the Rocks*'
189 × 120 cm

In front of a grotto the Virgin kneels protecting St John the Baptist with one hand and indicating the pre-eminence of the Christ Child with the other. An angel supports the Christ Child, who blesses the Baptist. St John, in representing the human race, is blessed by the Saviour and protected by the Virgin, who represents Mother Church.

The evolution of the artist's design for the picture is suggested by a sheet of drawings, now in the Metropolitan Museum of New York. At first (top right) the Virgin was shown kneeling with both hands folded gazing upon the Christ Child. This was a traditional concept for a painting of the Nativity. Then (top left) one of the Virgin's arms was extended and

(bottom left) both arms extended over the Child; finally (centre) a second child was introduced to give coherence to the pose of the Virgin with both arms outstretched.

This strange and magical altarpiece is made all the more so because, although pictures by Leonardo da Vinci are rare, there exists in the Louvre another picture almost identical in design and size to it. Scholars remain divided on the questions of whether both are by Leonardo and how they originated. The altarpiece was originally commissioned from Leonardo for the church of S. Francesco Grande in Milan in 1483, but in 1508 it was still unfinished. The London picture (which is unfinished) was removed from S. Francesco Grande in the eighteenth century. The history of the Louvre version can only be traced back to 1625 when it was seen at Fontainebleau, but it is generally agreed to be not only the earlier but also the finer of the two versions.

Studies by Leonardo da Vinci for the *Virgin of the Rocks*
(Metropolitan Museum, New York)

Study by Leonardo da Vinci for *The Virgin and Child with St Anne* (British Museum)

LEONARDO DA VINCI (1452–1519)
Cartoon: *The Virgin and Child with St Anne and St John the Baptist*
141.5 × 104.6 cm

The subject of the Cartoon, which Leonardo is known to have treated at least three times, is a combination of two themes, particularly associated with fifteenth-century Florentine painting: the Virgin and Child with St Anne (the mother of the Virgin) and the Virgin and Child with St John the Baptist.

In Leonardo's Cartoon the inclusion of St John suggests the earthly mission of Christ whose forerunner he was, while St Anne in pointing heavenward indicates that it was by God's will that Christ was born in order to save sinners.

The evolution of Leonardo's design for the Cartoon, which was probably drawn in the late 1490s, can be traced in a drawing now in the British Museum. The small drawings on the

bottom of the sheet show that the Virgin was originally placed cross-legged on the knees of St Anne and that Leonardo also experimented with the position of the Christ Child. It was only after many corrections and changes to the main drawing on the sheet that the final form of the design was established.

The Cartoon (from the Italian *cartone*, meaning large paper) has a haunting and evocative beauty. St Anne, almost the same age as her daughter, looks towards her with a strange and secret smile. In turn the Virgin looks at the Christ Child who blesses the Baptist. The particularly tender treatment of the subject, and the fact that both women are of similar age, led Sigmund Freud to relate Leonardo's fondness for the theme to the artist's own personal life. Leonardo was illegitimate and, it is supposed, spent the early years of his life with his peasant mother, but later was 'adopted' by his father's wife. Thus, in a sense, he had two mothers, the Virgin and St Anne of his pictures.

AGNOLO BRONZINO (1503–72)
An Allegory
146 × 116 cm

Vasari described this picture as one 'of singular beauty that was sent to King Francis I in France, wherein was a nude Venus, with Cupid who was kissing her, and Pleasure on one side with Folly and other Loves, and on the other side Fraud and Jealousy and other passions of love'. In the picture Cupid is indeed beguiled by the kiss of his mother Venus as she seeks to equip herself with his powers by robbing the arrow from his quiver. Jealousy tears her hair in anguish, while the head above her upon closer scrutiny is seen to be nothing more than a hollow mask and is therefore probably Fraud. The girl in the green dress, half animal, half human, is Pleasure, and proffering a honeycomb in one hand and the sting from her tail in the other, reminds us of the dual aspect of her nature: the sweetness she brings may also lead

to pain. The *putto* who prepares to shower the couple with roses is Folly. The aged winged figure, top right, is Time, and just as Venus disarms Cupid, so too does Time (by reaching for her drapery) attempt to disarm Fraud.

The subject of the picture is therefore a traditional one, Cupid disarmed by Venus; but in Bronzino's painting it is not through force, but rather through sweetness that Venus achieves her victory: the pillow on which Cupid kneels may, as in other paintings, signify flattery. By holding the golden apple awarded her by Paris, Venus reminds us of another contest in which she was also victorious.

The picture was probably painted some time in the 1540s. Bronzino was a Florentine, a pupil of Pontormo and much influenced by Michelangelo. About ten years before it was painted Michelangelo had made a cartoon for a nude *Venus kissing Cupid*, and a painting after that cartoon was made by Pontormo.

can be little doubt but that Venus in the Louvre picture is earthly and intended to represent profane love, while in the London painting she is winged and celestial, and her son, by discarding his bow and arrows, has renounced sensual love in favour of learning.

X-ray photographs show that the artist altered the positions of the heads of both Venus and Mercury, and he may originally have intended to show Mercury standing. The picture's compositional relationship to a Renaissance Holy Family, with a standing Mercury in the place of St Joseph, would then have been more obvious than it is today.

x-ray photograph

ANTONIO ALLEGRI DA CORREGGIO
(active 1514, d. 1534)
Mercury instructing Cupid before Venus
155 × 91 cm

Winged Venus has brought her son Cupid to be taught reading by Mercury. It would have been more usual for Mercury to instruct Cupid in the use of those weapons of love, his bow and arrows; but Correggio's translation of the theme into one of 'learning' would have appealed more to the Renaissance mind.

The picture, which was probably painted about 1520/25 for a member of the Gonzaga family at Mantua, is in all likelihood intended to represent more than just education. Its possible pendant from the same collection is a picture now in the Louvre, which shows Venus being gazed upon lustfully by a satyr as she lies asleep with her son Cupid. Together the two pictures were probably intended to convey the dual aspects of love, sacred and profane. There

MICHELANGELO (1475–1564)
The Entombment
161.7 × 149.9 cm

The painting (which is unfinished) shows the body of Christ being carried to the tomb after the Crucifixion. The figure supporting Christ on the spectator's right is probably St John; the bearer on the left is St Mary Magdalen; the outlined figure, bottom right, is possibly intended for the Virgin. The other female figure is either Mary Salome or Mary the sister of Martha. It seems likely that the unpainted area, to right, shows the tomb with two figures preparing it.

Michelangelo, by whom only one authenticated panel painting is known, the so-called '*Doni Tondo*' in the Uffizi, was also an architect and sculptor. The present picture is accepted as his work by most, though not all, scholars. In his treatment of the anatomy of the figures, and the tensions produced as they strain to support the dead weight of Christ, the artist would almost seem to be painting a sculptural group.

The picture is in oil and seems likely to have been painted in two stages. The two figures on the spectator's left are much more smoothly painted and accord best with the artist's earlier work, while the remaining finished parts of the picture employ a broader technique. Compositionally the picture owes much to the famous Antique marble group of the *Laocoön* which was discovered in Rome at a time when Michelangelo was also working in the city. The writhing serpents, which in the sculpture envelop the figures of Laocoön and his sons, are paralleled in the painting by the linen bands used to support the figure of Christ, and Christ's right foot rests on the step in a manner similar to Laocoön's. The *Laocoön* was discovered in January 1506 and Michelangelo is known to have left Rome suddenly in April of the same year. It is very likely that the earlier parts of *The Entombment* were painted before his sudden flight.

The Laocoön. Antique marble group of the 2nd–1st century BC (The Vatican Museum)

ANDREA DEL SARTO (1486–1530)
Portrait of a young Man
72.4 × 57 cm
Signed with the artist's monogram

The identity of the sitter in this hauntingly evocative portrait remains as elusive as the gaze of the sitter himself. It was originally identified at the Gallery as a self-portrait, and indeed the pose and stare conform well with those usually found in artists' self-portraits. But as a supposed self-portrait is known which is quite unlike the present sitter, this identification is now disregarded. Later the picture was called a *'Portrait of a Sculptor'* and the object in his hands was thought to be a block of stone, but this possibility is also now discounted.

The design of the picture is outstanding, with the sitter seated at an angle and almost with his back to the spectator. The understated colouring and diffused lighting enhance the introspective and contemplative quality of the sitter. This is characteristic of the painter, who, more than any other Florentine artist in the early sixteenth century, was influenced by the Venetians. After the departure of Michelangelo and Raphael for Rome in the first decade of the sixteenth century, Andrea became (with Fra Bartolomeo) the most important artist working in Florence.

PARMIGIANINO (1503–40)
The Mystic Marriage of St Catherine
74.2 × 57.2 cm

The subject is derived from *The Golden Legend*, where it is recorded that in a vision St Catherine of Alexandria was mystically married to Christ. The saint is recognizable by her attribute of the spiked wheel on which she was martyred. The head at the bottom left, probably that of some saint, cannot be identified with certainty.

The picture is possibly that which Vasari described as painted by Parmigianino for a close friend with whom he lodged at Bologna

between 1527 and 1531; but soon thereafter it was probably acquired by Cardinal Scipione Borghese in Rome.

Parmigianino, as his name implies, came from Parma, and his style was naturally influenced by that of Correggio, much of whose work was to be seen there. The composition of the present picture, and certain details such as the bearded head at the bottom, are derived from Correggio; but Parmigianino also refers to other High Renaissance artists, including Raphael and Michelangelo; he would have seen their work at Rome before he was forced to flee the city when German troops sacked it in 1527.

Pope Julius II by Raphael
(Chatsworth, Derbyshire)

RAPHAEL (1483–1520)
Pope Julius II
108 × 80.7 cm

RAPHAEL (1483–1520)
Altarpiece: *Madonna and Child with the Baptist and St Nicholas of Bari ('The Ansidei Madonna')*
209.6 × 148.6 cm

This is one of the pictures bought at the time of the foundation of the National Gallery in 1824; but until it was cleaned in 1970 it was thought to be no more than an old copy of a lost original. It is now recognized as Raphael's original portrait and it is in very good condition. It was painted in Rome in 1511/12 – the only years in which the Pope is known to have worn a beard. A drawing for the Pope's head is at Chatsworth.

The Della Rovere Pope Julius II (1433–1513) was the first great patron of Michelangelo, from whom he commissioned both a tomb for himself and the ceiling of the Sistine Chapel. He also employed Raphael to decorate the celebrated Stanze in the Vatican and Bramante to rebuild St Peter's.

This is an altarpiece, in exceptionally good condition, probably painted by Raphael in 1505 for the chapel of the Ansidei family in the church of S. Fiorenzo at Perugia. It was removed from the church in 1764 when it was bought through Gavin Hamilton by the family of the Duke of Marlborough, from whom it was purchased by the National Gallery in 1885 for the then unprecedented sum of £70,000.

The enthroned Madonna directs the attention of the Christ Child to the open book on her knee. The throne is inscribed *Salve Mater Christi*, and the Baptist points towards the Christ Child indicating His pre-eminence. As the Ansidei family chapel was dedicated to St Nicholas of Bari, he too is included in the altarpiece. The gold balls at his feet refer to the episode when the saint provided dowries for the three daughters of an impoverished nobleman by throwing a bag of gold for each through their father's window at night.

TITIAN (active before 1511, d. 1576)
Bacchus and Ariadne
175 × 190 cm
Signed: TICIANVS F.

Ariadne, the daughter of the King of Crete, was abandoned on the island of Naxos by Theseus. Several classical authors describe how, while wandering distractedly along the seashore and wearing an ungirt tunic she was surprised by the god Bacchus, who, leaping from his cheetah-drawn chariot, threw her crown to the heavens (thereby creating a constellation) and instantly promised her marriage. In his train he brought satyrs and bacchantes and the drunken Silenus on an ass. His followers, some girt with writhing snakes, variously carried tambourines and cymbals and the limbs of a slaughtered heifer.

Before Titian's time the subject was relatively

rare in Italian art. The right-hand side of the painting is compositionally recognizable as a Triumph, with excited revellers bearing trophies. The animation of this part of the picture is in contrast to the empty left-hand side where Bacchus and Ariadne gaze at one another against a clear background. Ariadne is startled and curious, Bacchus is instantaneously infatuated, but as yet only the foremost of Bacchus' train is even aware of Ariadne's presence. In an instant the lovers will be united and the revellers' dance will cease.

The picture was commissioned by Duke Alfonso I d'Este as one of a series of pictures of bacchanalian subjects intended to adorn a small room in his castle at Ferrara. Another picture which is known to have come from the same room is *The Feast of the Gods* by Giovanni Bellini (now in Washington) which was partly repainted by the young Titian. A *Worship of*

Venus and a *Bacchanal of the Andrians*, both by Titian and now in the Prado, were also part of the same series. The *Bacchus and Ariadne* was probably largely painted in Venice in the summer of 1522 and dispatched to Ferrara on 30 January 1523, where it was completed by Titian in the spring of that year.

TITIAN (active before 1511, d. 1576)
The Vendramin Family
205.7 × 301 cm

The two principal sitters in the portrait, which was probably painted in the early 1540s, are the brothers Gabriel (who gestures with his right hand towards the spectator) and Andrea Vendramin. The other men are the seven sons of Andrea. The family are shown on the steps of an altar and in adoration of a cross, although the more youthful sitters, who are either bored by or unaware of the significance of the setting, devote their attention to a pet dog. Being an all-male portrait-group (Andrea's six daughters are excluded from it) the picture has dynastic connotations. The oldest sitter, Andrea, as well as one of the youngest, by glancing at the spectator, remind us of age and youth, and

the fact that more than one generation is represented.

The significance of the painting is related to the cross on the altar. This was from the Scuola di San Giovanni Evangelista in Venice (it is still there) and contained a relic of the True Cross on which Christ was crucified. An ancestor of the Vendramin family (also Andrea, and the first to be ennobled) had been Guardiano of the Scuola in the fourteenth century and had received the cross as a gift on behalf of the Confraternity. Shortly afterwards when it was being carried in procession the cross almost fell into a canal, but was miraculously suspended above the water until Andrea Vendramin rescued it. On a later occasion when Andrea Vendramin prayed to it his cargo ships were saved during a storm at sea. Titian's portrait, therefore, is a proud statement of the family's veneration for the cross and as it shows more than one generation in adoration of it, it suggests that the Vendramin family will continue to invoke its protection.

The composition of the painting is striking with the principal figures, the cross and the flickering candles silhouetted against the sky, high above the spectator.

TITIAN (active before 1511, d. 1576)
Portrait of a Lady ('La Schiavona')
119.4 × 96.5 cm

The identity of the sitter in this portrait, which, on the evidence of the costume, was probably painted about 1511, is unknown; but as early as 1641 she was referred to as 'La Schiavona' – the Slav woman. She rests her left hand on a marble parapet which bears a relief profile portrait of herself. On the parapet are inscribed the letters T.V., probably referring to the artist 'Titianus Vecellius'.

The raised parapet is an afterthought, since her left sleeve is painted underneath it, and folds in the drapery are confused with veins in the marble. Titian also made other changes to the composition. Originally there was a circular 'window' in the top right-hand corner, but this was later painted out by the artist himself. Titian's paint was removed in an early restoration of the portrait and the window area again inpainted by the restorer. That alteration was removed at the National Gallery in 1959/60, when a new restoration of the area was made.

X-ray photographs reveal an elliptical shape in the area now occupied by the profile relief. On the basis of comparison with other portraits by Titian, this shape could originally have been intended as a dish held by an attendant page.

x-ray photograph of *La Schiavona*

La Schiavona photographed during restoration

LORENZO LOTTO (*c.* 1480–after 1556)
A Lady as Lucretia
95.9 × 110.5 cm

The portrait was originally in the Palazzo Pesaro in Venice and the lady depicted is probably Lucrezia Valier, who married Benedetto Pesaro in 1533. The costume would indicate that it was painted either just before or very soon after her marriage. As she is Lucrezia she points to the drawing of her Roman namesake, Lucretia, which she holds in her left hand. The Roman Lucretia, a virtuous woman who committed suicide after being raped is a traditional symbol for chastity. In Lotto's portrait, therefore, Lucrezia Pesaro consciously asserts her own virtue. The note on the table is

inscribed: NEC VLLA IMPVDICA LUCRETIAE EXEMPLO VIVET ('after Lucretia's example let no violated woman live').

The portrait is painted not without wit – both on the part of the painter and the sitter: there is no reason to suppose that Lucrezia Pesaro was anything but virtuous, but she willingly allows Lotto to proclaim her virtuousness in a manner which serves only to arouse our suspicions.

Lotto was probably a Venetian by birth, but worked at various centres in the north of Italy and also in Rome. His style is highly original and individual. In this picture the composition, with the sitter highlighted against a blank background and 'leaning out' towards the spectator, is dramatic, and of a type which is known to have had an influence on the young Caravaggio.

PAOLO VERONESE
(born probably 1528, d. 1588)
The Family of Darius before Alexander
236 × 474 cm

After the Battle of Issus, Alexander the Great and his friend Hephaestion visited the family of his defeated enemy, Darius. The mother of Darius, supposing Hephaestion, who was the taller of the two, to be Alexander, offered him the obeisance due to the victorious monarch. Alexander magnanimously forgave her by saying of Hephaestion that he too was Alexander. In Veronese's picture it is by no means clear which of the two principal figures is Alexander. At first sight it is natural to take him to be the more prominent figure in red who gestures towards his companion; but the latter gestures towards himself, and as his armour is decorated with laurel, it may be that he is the victorious Alexander.

An eighteenth-century account suggests that the picture was painted (probably in the 1570s) for a member of the Pisani family of Venice in return for hospitality received by the artist, possibly at the Pisani villa at Este. It is further thought that many of the principal figures in the picture are portraits of members of the family.

Veronese's crowded, sumptuous and pageant-like canvasses suggest the splendour of sixteenth-century Venice. Part of that splendour was the architecture of Andrea Palladio and Sansovino, and it is from a typically Venetian colonnade in the background that figures lean to glimpse the scene taking place in the foreground of the picture.

PAOLO VERONESE
(born probably 1528, d. 1588)
A series: *An Allegory of Love*
Each canvas about 186 × 186 cm

The original setting of these four paintings, which probably decorated a ceiling, is not known. They once belonged to the Holy Roman Emperor, Rudolf II, at Prague and later to Queen Christina of Sweden. They came to England in the 1790s. The four pictures may be interpreted generally as allegories illustrating themes on the pleasures and pains of love. In one picture Cupid chastises a naked man while Chastity, carrying a white ermine, leads a lady away. In the background are statues of Pan, with his pipes and a satyr – both emblems of lust. In another picture Cupid, his arrow held aloft, leads a man towards the bed of a naked and possibly drunken woman (an empty beaker is beside her bed). A third picture shows a woman who probably represents Supreme Pleasure, as she is represented naked except for pearls and is seated on silk. This woman is shown as the conqueror of both active and contemplative man – the one is dressed in armour, while the other seems inspired by music. The final picture shows a couple, both

fully clothed and holding together an olive branch, symbol of peace, and crowned, by a figure who is possibly Fortune, accompanied by a cornucopia and enthroned on a sphere. Cupid holds a conjugal chain, and a dog, symbol of fidelity, looks on.

JACOPO TINTORETTO (1518–94)
St George and the Dragon
157.5 × 100.3 cm

The subject of St George and the Dragon, which is half historical, half legend, was a popular one with painters of all periods and there are several other versions in the National Gallery. Characteristically, Tintoretto's version is more agitated and dramatic than most others. The saint drives his lance into the dragon while the princess stumbles towards the spectator in her flight. Tintoretto received many commissions from the Church in his native Venice and was himself religious. In this painting he brings a religious significance to the story of St George. The princess seems to be saved by Divine intervention: God the Father appears in a radiance in the sky, while the dragon's earlier victim lies on the ground in an attitude which suggests the crucified Christ. The picture may have been commissioned as a private altarpiece, but it is not known for whom. It was possibly painted some time in the 1560s.

JACOPO TINTORETTO (1518–94)
The Origin of the Milky Way
148 × 165 cm

Jupiter, wishing to immortalize the infant
Hercules, whose mother was the mortal Alc-
mene, fed him at the breast of the sleeping
goddess Juno. According to the legend, lilies
sprouted where Juno's milk fell to earth, and
the stars of the Milky Way appeared where the
milk spilled heavenward. This account of the
origin of the lily was given in a Byzantine
botanical textbook, *Geoponica*, of which Italian
translations were published in Venice in 1542
and 1549; and it is probably from that book
that Tintoretto's treatment of the theme is
derived. Juno is attended by her peacock and
Jupiter by his eagle, bearing a thunderbolt. A
putto carries a net, symbol of deceit, while
others hold erotic symbols such as a flaming
torch, a bow and arrows.

The earthly lilies are not visible in the
National Gallery picture, which has been cut at
some time. The original appearance of the
painting is recorded in sketches by other artists
which show that a figure representing Earth
once occupied the bottom part of the painting,
where lilies were also depicted.

The Origin of the Milky Way drawn by an unknown artist
after the picture by Tintoretto. (Accademia, Venice)

The picture, which probably belongs to the
1570s, may have been painted for the Emperor
Rudolf II in Prague. Mythological paintings by
Tintoretto are relatively rare; the majority of
his pictures, which are often on a vast scale, are
of religious subjects and were mostly commissioned either by the Church or State in Venice.

Ascribed to NICCOLO DELL'ABATE
(*c.* 1509/12–71)
The Story of Aristaeus
189 × 237.5 cm

Several episodes from the classical story of the shepherd Aristaeus are shown taking place simultaneously in the picture. In the foreground Aristaeus is pursuing Eurydice (who is also depicted dead on the ground) while to the right he consults with his mother Cyrene. Orpheus, in the middle distance, charms the wild animals with the music from his lyre.

The artist's treatment of the story is as fanciful and fantastic as the landscape in which it takes place. In the background a cool and unreal city with palaces, temples, towers and spires miraculously clings to the jagged coastline of some weird and elegant land.

Niccolo dell'Abate was born in Modena in northern Italy, and in his painting of landscape was probably influenced by the work of Dosso Dossi, who worked in neighbouring Ferrara. His treatment of figures owed much to the Mannerist style of Parmigianino, who worked in Parma. By 1552 Niccolo was painting in France in the service of the Crown, and it was in the decoration of the château of the French kings at Fontainebleau that he developed a highly individual and decorative style, which he shared with other Italian artists also working at Fontainebleau – Francesco Primaticcio and Giovanni Battista Rosso among them. This school of painting is referred to as the First School of Fontainebleau.

ADAM ELSHEIMER (1578–1610)
St Lawrence prepared for Martyrdom
26.7 × 20.6 cm

Elsheimer was a German artist whose minutely painted small pictures on copper were to prove enormously influential for later seventeenth-century painters. By 1600 he had settled in Rome and it was almost certainly after that date that this picture was painted: the building in the background is based on the ruins of the Temple of Vespasian in the Roman Forum and the statue of Hercules is vaguely derived from the Farnese *Hercules* then recently discovered in Rome.

St Lawrence was martyred by being roasted on a gridiron for refusing to reveal the supposed treasures of the Church, but in this picture Elsheimer seems to imply that the saint was martyred for refusing to worship pagan idols.

ANNIBALE CARRACCI (1560–1609)
'The Three Maries'
92.8 × 103 cm

It is after the Crucifixion and the body of Christ has been removed from the Cross. He is mourned by the Virgin (who supports Him), the Magdalen (towards his feet) and two other women who are probably Mary Salome and Mary the mother of James. The subject therefore is not quite either of the traditional themes of *Pietà* or *Lamentation,* which show the Virgin alone with her dead son or with the other Maries and St John the Evangelist. X-radiographs and *pentimenti* reveal several extra figures underneath the picture; and as they are painted at right angles to the figures which are visible they seem to suggest that the artist originally intended to use the canvas for a different upright composition.

The picture was probably painted about 1604, that is, fairly late in the artist's career, and at a time when he had just finished, after some seven years' work, his masterpiece: the frescoed decoration of the Gallery of the Farnese Palace, Rome. Annibale had settled in Rome in 1595, having moved there from Bologna, where, with other members of his family, he had established a famous teaching Academy in the 1580s. The teaching in that Academy was based largely on a revaluation of the ideals of the High Renaissance, but Annibale was also particularly influenced by the work of Correggio, which he would have seen in neighbouring Parma. Bellori, an early biographer of Annibale, wrote: 'One cannot insist enough on the extent to which Annibale penetrated and took possession of Correggio's style – of his composition and of the expression of his figures'. The present picture indeed owes much in composition to a painting by Correggio, still at Parma.

Although the painting is not mentioned in any of the early literature on Annibale, it has been one of the most famous of the artist's works since the eighteenth century. The design was used early in the eighteenth century for a Gobelins tapestry; Diderot referred to it as 'une des plus sublimes compositions du Carrache'; and at the Manchester Exhibition of 1857 (the most gigantic art exhibition ever) the picture was the most popular of all the paintings exhibited.

x-ray photograph of *The Three Maries*
by Annibale Carracci

DOMENICHINO (1581–1641)
Landscape with Tobias laying hold of the Fish
45 × 33.9 cm

Tobias, having been attacked by a great fish while bathing in the River Tigris, was instructed by his companion, the Archangel Raphael, to catch the fish and gut it. Tobias later used the fish's gall to cure the blindness of his father Tobit.

In the very foreground of the painting, and framed by tall trees, the Archangel and Tobias enact their story; but the real subject of the picture is the beautiful landscape which recedes behind them. Splashes of white in the river lead the eye through the middle distance towards the far hill-top towns. As the landscape becomes more remote it becomes lighter, and the sky settles on the horizon with a pink glow.

As a young man, Domenichino trained in the Bolognese Academy of the Carracci family and came to Rome in 1602 to work with Annibale Carracci on the decoration of the Farnese Palace. Most of his more important commissions were for altarpieces and the frescoed decoration of churches, mainly in Rome and Naples; but perhaps his most important contribution as a painter was his development of the type of classical landscape as seen in the present picture. Annibale too painted such landscapes, and the work of both artists influenced, later in the seventeenth century, the greatest of all classical landscape painters, Claude Lorraine.

MICHELANGELO MERISI DA CARAVAGGIO
(1571–1610)
The Supper at Emmaus
141 × 196 cm

The story of the Supper at Emmaus is told only
in St Luke's Gospel. After the Resurrection two
of the disciples, Cleophas and another, un-
named, were overtaken on the road to Emmaus
by a stranger who walked with them until
evening. Upon reaching an inn, the disciples
invited the stranger to sup with them, and
when at supper He took bread, blessed it,
broke it and gave it to them (as at the Last
Supper) they recognized Him as their Master.

The Subject was a traditional one in art and
many versions of it are known from the late
fifteenth century onwards. In comparison with
earlier treatments of the theme Caravaggio's
picture is revolutionary, and it influenced (as
most of his pictures did) an enormous number
of artists later in the seventeenth century. The
scene portrayed is dramatic, immediate and

extremely naturalistic, and on looking at the
picture the spectator becomes involved in the
moment of recognition in a way that the artist
intended he should be. The dramatic lighting
draws our attention: the table, painted close-to,
puts the scene in focus, and the blank background does not lead the eye away from the
figures. Such details as the torn sleeve of
Cleophas, the outstretched arm of the other
disciple and the basket of fruit about to topple
from the table make the picture-space an
extension of the space in which the spectator is
standing. Symbolism plays its part. The bread
and wine suggest the Eucharist, the pome-
granate is a symbol of Resurrection, and the
piercing light may be the light of salvation.
The scallop shell is the emblem of the pilgrim,
for traditionally the disciples at Emmaus were
depicted as pilgrims.

The picture is a youthful work by the artist
and was possibly painted about 1602 in Rome.
It is the earlier of two versions of the subject by
him.

PHILIPPE DE CHAMPAIGNE (1602–74)
Cardinal Richelieu
259.7 × 177.8 cm
Inscribed: *P. de Champaigne*

There are several versions of this portrait of
Cardinal Richelieu, who was Chief Minister of
France under Louis XIII and who died in 1642.
These portraits would have been painted as
gifts and were based on a standard image of
Richelieu which he approved in 1640.

NICOLAS POUSSIN (1594?–1665)
Landscape with a Man killed by a Snake
119.4 × 198.8 cm

Poussin's landscapes, in contrast to those of
Claude, his great French contemporary in
Rome, have an almost two-dimensional quality. All the elements of the composition are
subordinated to an overall surface pattern. The
forms of the architecture assume geometric
proportions – an effect which is enhanced when
buildings are reflected in water. This picture,
probably painted in 1648, may show the plain
and town of Fondi, between Rome and Naples,
which Poussin is known to have seen. The
plain of Fondi was notorious for the snakes
which infested it, and the scene in the painting
may have been inspired by an incident which
the painter witnessed. Poussin's picture may
also be intended to express the various states of
fear: the running man is more frightened than
the woman, who in turn is more frightened
than the fisherman in the boat.

CLAUDE (1600–82)
Seaport: The Embarkation of the Queen of Sheba
148.6 × 193.7 cm
Signed: *Claude Gl. i.v. facit. por. son. altesse. le dvc. de. Bvillon a Romae. 1648*

Throughout his life Claude was attracted by the subject of seaport scenes. Another picture in the National Gallery shows the embarkation of St Ursula; but in the present picture it is the Queen of Sheba who embarks for the court of King Solomon. By placing the sun low in the distant sky, Claude was able to paint the effects of light falling on water, architecture and ship's rigging. The buildings to right and left and in the middle distance perform the same function in the composition as do the trees in Claude's views of the Roman Campagna (see p. 96): that is, they lead the eye into the picture towards the horizon.

Claude's pictures became very popular during his lifetime and from about 1635 he recorded them in drawings which he retained as a precaution against forgeries or copies. Collected together in a book called the *Liber Veritatis*, they are now in the British Museum.

There is a similar picture to this in the Doria-Pamphilj collection in Rome, and the picture is also recorded in the *Liber Veritatis*. The drawing is inscribed *quadro faict per lexellent^{me} Sig principe panfil*, but, nevertheless, it is clear that it is the National Gallery composition which is the one recorded.

The Embarkation of the Queen of Sheba. Drawing by Claude from the *Liber Veritatis*. (British Museum)

95

CLAUDE (1600–82)
The Marriage of Isaac and Rebekah ('The Mill')
149 × 196 cm
Signed: CLVDIO . G.L.
   I.N.V. ROMAE 1648/F

The artist has inscribed a title for the picture in French on the tree stump in the centre. It reads: MARI (age) DISAC AVEC REBECA. Abraham, the father of Isaac, sent his servant Eleizer to find a suitable bride for his son. When Rebekah gave Eleizer and his camels water from a well (the scene most usually depicted by artists) he brought her back to Canaan as Isaac's bride. Claude's picture shows figures dancing and celebrating in a beautiful landscape, but which of the figures is Isaac or Rebekah is as irrelevant as is the title itself.

The real subject of the picture is the beautiful landscape. Claude was a French painter who went to Italy at about the age of thirteen and spent almost all his life in Rome. Influenced by such artists as Elsheimer and Paul Brill, he created a type of poetic classical landscape in paint which was to influence landscape painters throughout Europe for over two centuries. Such pictures were inspired by the Roman Campagna and by the remains of classical ruins which the artist could have seen there. A sense of tremendous distance is created by the placing of trees or buildings in diminishing scale on either side of the composition, and some feature (such as the mill in the present picture) is used to set the middle distance. The view is unified by the use of colour with a dark brown/green foreground, a light green middle distance and a pale blue horizon which blends into the sky.

NICOLAS POUSSIN (?1594–1665)
The Adoration of the Golden Calf
154 × 214 cm

Moses, when leading the Israelites out of
Egypt into Canaan, ascended Mount Sinai and
received from God the Tablets of the Law.
Upon returning and discovering the Israelites
worshipping an idol, the Golden Calf which
Aaron had fashioned for them out of golden
ornaments, Moses cast the stone tablets to the
ground and broke them. The picture, with its
pendant, *The Crossing of the Red Sea* (now in
Melbourne), was painted, probably about
1635/7, for Amadeo dal Pozzo, a cousin of one
of the artist's most famous patrons, Cassiano
dal Pozzo.

All the people in the picture are shown in
action, the dancing figures forming a frieze in
front of the statue and the other groups all
gesturing towards it. In spite of this, however,
the picture has a very static quality, and upon
closer scrutiny the figures seem almost frozen
in movement. The same effect is apparent in
another Poussin in the National Gallery, the
Bacchanalian Revel before a Term of Pan (page
203), where indeed many of the dancers adopt
the same poses.

Poussin was born in Normandy and spent
his early years in Paris, but settled in Rome
when he was thirty, returning to France on
only one occasion for about eighteen months in
1641/2. In contrast to the Baroque style of most
contemporary painters working in Rome,
Poussin's paintings are noticeably classical, and
are influenced by both Raphael and the Antique. In the present picture the group of the
mother with her children is a Raphaelesque
Charity, and the frieze of figures is not unlike
that on an Antique sarcophagus. In his earlier
paintings Poussin had been influenced by
Venetian colour, but the influences apparent in
the present picture became more important to
him from the 1630s onwards.

Drawing by Rubens for the figure of Hymen
(Albertina, Vienna)

PETER PAUL RUBENS (1577–1640)
Minerva protects Pax from Mars
203 × 298 cm

Helmeted Minerva rebuffs Mars, God of War, while a nude female figure representing Pax (Peace) feeds with milk from her breast a child who is Plutus, God of Wealth. Youthful Hymen, God of Marriage, bearing a torch, crowns a young girl. A satyr offers fruits from a cornucopia and a female figure brings in objects of luxury. A *putto* in the sky brings an olive wreath and a caduceus, symbols of Peace and Concord. The picture is therefore conventionally allegorical. It represents the benefits of peace. Wealth grows, marriage flourishes, while Plenty and Luxury are also in evidence.

But Rubens intended a more specific meaning than that. In June 1629 he came to England as the envoy of Philip IV of Spain. Throughout his career he acted as diplomat as well as being a painter. His mission was to negotiate a peace treaty between England and Spain, and in this he was ultimately successful. He was later knighted by Charles I and left England in May 1632. It was during his stay in England and while the negotiations for peace were proceed-

ing that he painted this picture which he presented to Charles I. It is fitting, therefore, that the benefits of Peace are shown as only being possible if Mars is successfully repulsed.

When in London Rubens lodged with one of Charles I's courtiers, Sir Balthasar Gerbier. The boy Hymen, and two of the girls which he protects in Rubens's picture, are portraits of three of Gerbier's children, based on drawings.

PETER PAUL RUBENS (1577–1640)
The Birth of Venus
61 × 78.1 cm

Venus, wringing the sea-foam from her hair with her right hand, steps ashore on the island of Cythera (or Cyprus). She is assisted by the Three Graces and crowned by Cupid and Persuasion while Desire, riding on a Triton, follows in her wake. In the outer border are (above) Neptune, God of the Sea, and Amphitrite and (below) Cupid and Psyche. The picture is probably a design by Rubens for the decoration of a dish which was subsequently made in silver for Charles I by Theodore Rogiers. The dish can no longer be traced, but an etching of it, and the ewer which accompanied it (and for which Rubens also made a design), was published in the seventeenth century.

The National Gallery's design, painted in grisaille to suggest the medium in which it would be executed, was probably painted in the early 1630s; on several occasions Rubens provided designs for sculptors in wood, stone and ivory as well as for silversmiths.

Etching by Jacob Neefs of a silver basin and ewer, the design for which was supplied by Rubens. (Teylers Museum, Haarlem)

PETER PAUL RUBENS (1577–1640)
The Château de Steen
131.8 × 229.9 cm

Five years before his death in 1640 at the age of
sixty-three, Rubens bought the Château de
Steen, and this view of the castle and surrounding landscape was probably painted soon
afterwards. The castle remains largely un-
altered today. Rubens's view is due north, the
town on the horizon is probably Antwerp and,
from the position of the sun, it is clear that it is
early morning. The flowering plants in the
hedgerow in the foreground indicate that it is
autumn.

The picture is a mass of detail with the
minutiae of country life – flowers, birds and
trees – lovingly and carefully portrayed. Black-
berry brambles, partridges, kingfishers, magpies
are all recognizable, and from the castle a
cart, laden with farm products, sets off to
market. The picture, probably more than any
other landscape which Rubens painted, is a
joyful celebration of country life and the
freedom which it offers, and it is as such that he
probably saw it himself.

Rubens, diplomat as well as painter, had led
an enormously active life and had travelled
continuously between the courts of Europe.

Now in his last years he lived in semi-retirement
at Steen, and it is not impossible that the
sportsman with the gun in the foreground is
intended to be a self-portrait.

PETER PAUL RUBENS (1577–1640)
Susanna Lunden ? ('Le Chapeau de Paille')
79 × 54/54.6 cm

Ever since Reynolds saw this portrait in
Antwerp in 1781, when he described it as '*The
Chapeau de Paille*', the picture has been thus
affectionately, but quite inaccurately, known.
The sitter is in fact wearing a felt hat similar to
others worn by both men and women in the
Netherlands in the early 1620s.

She is most probably Susanna Fourment
(1599–1643), the third daughter of an Antwerp
silk and tapestry merchant. She was widowed
at an early age and re-married in 1622, when
her husband was Arnold Lunden. Her youngest sister, Helena, married Rubens (as his
second wife) in 1630.

It was not unusual for people to have
betrothal portraits painted, and Susanna
Lunden's age and costume would seem to

suggest that the picture was painted at the time of her second marriage in 1622: the ring she wears on the first finger of her right hand is almost certainly a wedding ring. Rubens was a friend of the Fourment family and very probably the affection with which the portrait was obviously painted accounts for its tremendous appeal and popularity. With her red dress dramatically juxtaposed against the wind-buffeted blue sky, Susanna Fourment shyly contemplates the spectator; and knowing her circumstances, about to embark on a second marriage, one sees in her glance a sense of joy and hope.

JACOB JORDAENS (1593–1678)
? *Govaert van Surpele and his wife*
23.4 × 188.9 cm

The armorial bearings in the picture identify the male sitter as a member of the Van Surpele family of Diest. It seems most likely that he is Govaert van Surpele (1593–1674) who held several important government positions. The portrait was probably commissioned to commemorate his appointment to some particular office, the emblem of which is the staff he holds in his right hand. As the sitter also wears a sword and sash it seems probable that the office was military rather than civil.

The portrait may also be a marriage picture, but as Govaert van Surpele was married twice, in 1614 to Catharina Cools (d. 1629) and in 1636 to Catharina Coninckx (d. 1639), it cannot be stated with certainty which of his two wives is included in the portrait, although the style of the picture and the age of the sitter would indicate that it was painted some time in the 1630s.

Jordaens worked in Antwerp, and was an assistant of Rubens. Van Dyck was the most fashionable portraitist in Antwerp after his return from Italy in about 1627, but in this portrait of a middle-aged couple Jordaens competes with him successfully and achieves something of the grandeur and assurance that one associates with the younger artist.

ANTHONY VAN DYCK (1599–1641)
The Abbot Scaglia adoring the Virgin and Child
106.7 × 120 cm

Representing the House of Savoy, the Abbot Scaglia played an active part in promoting peace between England and Spain in the 1620s. Subsequently, because of his anti-French sympathies, he fell out of favour with the Duke of Savoy and from 1632 he lived in retirement at Brussels. It was probably soon thereafter that this picture was painted; and as the Virgin in the painting bears a strong resemblance to the Duchess of Savoy, the picture may have been commissioned by Scaglia as part of the efforts which he is known to have made to establish better relations between himself and the family.

The composition of the painting is based on a lost picture by Titian which Van Dyck saw in Italy in the 1620s and recorded in his Italian sketchbook (now in the British Museum).

The Virgin and Child with a donor by Van Dyck after Titian.
(British Museum)

DIEGO VELÁZQUEZ (1599–1660)
Philip IV of Spain in Brown and Silver
195 × 110 cm
Signed, on the paper in his right hand: *Senor.
Diego Velasquz. Pintor de V. Mg.*

Philip IV (1605–65) was King of Spain from
1621 and appointed Velázquez as his Court
Painter in 1623. Between 1631 and 1635
Velázquez painted several portraits of the
King, of which this is one. As it is signed (and
only a few of the painter's pictures are) it would
seem that Velázquez considered it to be
particularly important. The signature is in the
form of a petition to the King from the painter.

ANTHONY VAN DYCK (1599–1641)
Equestrian Portrait of Charles I
367 × 292 cm

The portrait is one of two equestrian portraits
in the National Gallery (the other is by
Rembrandt) and one of two such portraits of
Charles I by Van Dyck: the other is at Windsor.
Charles I became King of Great Britain and
Ireland in 1625. His rule led to civil war and to
his own execution.

The King, who is identified by a tablet
hanging on the tree behind him which reads
CAROLVS REX MAGNAE BRITANIAE, is shown in
armour similar to that made in the royal
workshops at Greenwich between 1610 and
1620. The decoration hanging on the gold
chain about his neck is the Lesser George. An
equerry to the right holds his helmet. The
breed of the King's horse has been the subject
of inconclusive speculation. It is thought to be
a 'great horse', but the possibility of its being
Flemish or Spanish has also been suggested. A
drawing in the British Museum for the horse
has an anonymous rider sketched in.

Charles I was possibly the greatest art patron
of all English monarchs. He assembled a noted
collection of paintings which was dispersed by

Study by Van Dyck for *Equestrian Portrait of Charles I*
(British Museum)

sale after his death. He patronized Rubens, and his appointment of the Flemish Van Dyck as his Court Painter in 1632 had almost immeasurable consequences for British painting. Van Dyck's portraits of the King and his courtiers form an elegant and exquisite record of that doomed court, and British portrait painters of later generations sought and found inspiration in Van Dyck when commissioned to paint later monarchs and their courtiers.

EL GRECO (1541–1614)
Christ driving the Traders from the Temple
106.3 × 129.7 cm

El Greco painted the subject of *Christ driving the Traders from the Temple* several times. For him and his contemporaries Christ's act of purification probably symbolized the Counter-Reformation movement to purge the Church of heresy. On the right-hand side of the picture are the redeemed, while to the left are the unredeemed traders, almost as in a *Last Judgment*. The dramatic figure of Christ in the centre is emphasized by the open arch behind Him, and the reliefs in the background, which show *The Expulsion from Paradise* and *The*

Sacrifice of Isaac, allude to the theme of the picture: *The Expulsion* refers to the unredeemed, while *The Sacrifice of Isaac* was an Old Testament prototype of the Crucifixion and therefore here stands for the Redemption.

El Greco ('the Greek') was born in Crete, and after some years working in Venice and Rome had settled at Toledo in Spain by 1577. He was much influenced by contemporary Italian painters; several of the poses in the present picture derive from Michelangelo, Raphael, Titian and Tintoretto. But his style was highly individual, both in colouring and in his intense, indeed ecstatic, treatment of mystical subjects. The National Gallery's *Christ driving the Traders from the Temple* was probably painted about 1600.

FRANCISCO DE ZURBARÁN (1598–1664)
St Margaret
163 × 105 cm

The Saint is here represented, in striking
contemporary costume, as a shepherdess, and
the picture may well be a portrait, not of a
shepherdess, but of a lady of fashion disguising
herself as one. Declaring herself a Christian
virgin, St Margaret refused to marry the

Prefect of Antioch and was thereupon thrown
into a dungeon, where she was devoured by
Satan in the form of a dragon. As she was
subsequently delivered when the dragon burst
open, she became the patron saint of pregnant
women, and as such enjoyed a certain popularity. This picture was probably painted in
the early 1630s, soon after Zurbarán, who was
popular as a painter of religious pictures,
settled in Seville.

DIEGO VELÁZQUEZ (1599–1660)
The Toilet of Venus ('*The Rokeby Venus*')
122 × 177 cm

This is the artist's only surviving painting of a female nude, a subject which is extremely rare in Spanish seventeenth-century painting (although Velázquez is known to have painted at least four). *The Rokeby Venus* is first recorded in 1651 when it hung, in a black frame, in the Madrid palace of the Marqués del Carpio, the son of Philip IV's First Minister. The picture came to England in 1813 and was sold soon afterwards to John Morritt of Rokeby Park in Yorkshire, from which it takes its name.

The picture may have been painted either shortly before, or during, Velázquez's second visit to Italy in 1649/51. Earlier, in 1629/31, he had also visited Italy, where he spent some time in Venice copying and studying the great

Venetian painters of the sixteenth century. Those painters, in particular Titian, had popularized such themes as a nude, reclining Venus, and Venus at a mirror attended by Cupid, and there were at least two such paintings by Titian in the Royal Palace, Madrid. In his painting Velázquez combines both themes, but makes of the picture something peculiarly his own. His nude Venus has a very different kind of beauty from that of the Venetian nudes of Titian.

The mirror in the picture is given special prominence and recalls for us the use of the mirror in another famous Velázquez, *Las Meninas*. In that picture the mirror reflects images of Philip IV and his Queen present in the painter's studio. In the *Rokeby Venus* the 'reflection' is unreal: held at such an angle the mirror would not reflect the face of Venus, and even if it did, it would show more than her head.

BARTOLOMÉ ESTEBAN MURILLO (1617–82)
Christ healing the Paralytic at the Pool of Bethesda
237 × 261 cm

The subject is taken from St John's Gospel, where it is recorded that those suffering from diseases would come to a pool (with five arches) in Jerusalem, called Bethesda. At a certain season an angel would descend into the pool and whoever stepped in thereafter would be miraculously cured. In Murillo's picture a paralysed man appeals to Jesus that he has no one to immerse him and Jesus replies, 'Rise, take up thy bed and walk' and the man is at that moment cured. The pool, with its classical arcade, appears in the background.

Murillo was accepted in 1665 as a member of the Confraternity which owned the hospital of La Caridad ('Charity') in Seville. Between 1667 and 1670 he painted a series of pictures for the church attached to it. This is one of them, illustrating Works of Mercy from the Bible. The pictures, which were already famous in the artist's lifetime, remained the most famous works of art in Seville until they were partially dispersed by Napoleon's commander in the Peninsula in 1810.

Murillo was born in Seville where he worked throughout his life. He only occasionally visited Madrid, where he came under the influence of Velázquez and also of the paintings of Van Dyck and Rubens in the Royal Collection.

REMBRANDT (1606–69)
Jacob Trip
130.5 × 97.2 cm
Signed: *Rembr*.

Jacob Trip (1575–1661) was a successful merchant from Dordrecht whose businesses included the manufacture of armaments. There are at least six other known portraits of him and many portraits of his wife (two by Rembrandt are in the National Gallery). As the Trips had at least twelve children it is probable that these numerous portraits were painted for their family. This portrait was probably painted in the last months of Jacob Trip's life, and possibly when he was on a visit to his son in Amsterdam where Rembrandt worked.

The picture is a fine and characteristic late portrait by the artist; and it has many of the qualities which now make the artist's portraits

so popular: colouring inspired by the Venetians, rich use of paint and above all a compassionate treatment of the sitter. From the 1640s Rembrandt's practice declined (he was once immensely successful) and in 1656 he was declared bankrupt. Knowing the troubled circumstances of the artist's own life, this portrait of the eighty-six-year-old Jacob Trip seems all the more moving.

REMBRANDT (1606–69)
Belshazzar's Feast
167.6 × 209.2 cm
Signed: *Rembrand. f 163*(?)

The subject is taken from the Old Testament Book of Daniel. The Hebrew writing on the wall, to be read vertically from right to left, foretells with the words *Mene, Mene Tekel Upharsin*, the downfall of Belshazzar and the kingdom of Babylon. At a banquet for his princes, wives and concubines, at which he used the precious vessels stolen from the Temple at Jerusalem, Belshazzar is astounded by the hand of God writing on the wall. As neither the King nor his sages could interpret the writing (for it is in a sort of code) the prophet Daniel was called upon to explain it to the King.

Rembrandt's form of the words, which in other paintings of the subject were either omitted or inscribed in Latin, probably indicates that the picture was painted for a Jewish patron. The formula employed by Rembrandt was probably suggested by a friend, Menassah Ben Israel; he published a book in Amsterdam in 1639 in which he argued that the writing on the wall was written, as here, in Hebrew from top to bottom and from right to left – a suggestion which was rejected by both Catholic and Protestant theologians.

The final digit of the dated signature is missing, but the picture is likely to have been painted after 1635, although not necessarily as late as 1639, the date of publication of Ben Israel's book.

Woman bathing in a Stream by Rembrandt

REMBRANDT (1606–69)
Hendrickje Stoffels
101.9 × 83.8 cm
Signed: *Rembrandt. f. 16 (?5) 9*

The sitter, Hendrickje Stoffels, was born about 1625 and from about 1649 was the artist's mistress (Rembrandt's wife, Saskia, had died in 1642). In July 1652 Hendrickje was summoned before the council of the Reformed Church and admonished for living in sin with Rembrandt. Later that year she bore him a daughter, Cornelia. The reason why Rembrandt never married Hendrickje is assumed to be because, by the terms of Saskia's will, he would have had to give up half his estate on remarriage. Hendrickje predeceased the artist by six years.

Although there is no documented portrait of Hendrickje by Rembrandt, she is generally supposed to be the model in several of his paintings executed in the 1650s: she is for example almost certainly the *Woman bathing in a Stream*, also in the National Gallery, and there are other portraits of her in Berlin, Bonn and the Louvre. A picture in the National Gallery of Scotland of a woman in bed is also generally supposed to represent Hendrickje.

Rembrandt, who was born in Leyden, set himself up in Amsterdam, probably in early 1632. By then he was already known and during the 1630s became enormously successful. After the death of his wife Saskia his business declined and, although he still received a number of commissions, he was eventually declared bankrupt in 1656. From 1660 onwards Hendrickje, together with his son Titus, 'employed' the artist, thus protecting him from his creditors. Later in life he received fewer portrait commissions and turned more often to biblical subjects and landscapes.

REMBRANDT *Saskia van Ulenborch* (detail). See page 114

REMBRANDT (1606–69)
Saskia van Ulenborch
123.5 × 97.5 cm
Traces of a false signature: *Rem(..) a(.) 1635*

Saskia van Ulenborch (1612–42) married Rembrandt in 1634. She was the daughter of a wealthy burgomaster of Leeuwarden and her cousin was an art-dealer in Amsterdam with whom Rembrandt lodged from 1632 probably until his marriage. Saskia brought the painter a large dowry, and bore him four children; but at her death at the age of thirty in 1642 only one son, Titus, survived.

The picture may have been at some time slightly reduced in size. The signature seems to be false, but it may well have been copied from one on the part of the picture which was removed. The date in the signature seems about right, as it accords well with the age of the sitter. The portrait also has stylistic

affinities with Rembrandt's other paintings of this time.

The picture has often been called *Saskia as Flora* – the Roman goddess of Spring and Flowers whom Titian characterized in a famous picture of a beautiful young girl holding a bouquet of flowers. It seems more likely, however, that Rembrandt was only depicting his young wife in a type of fanciful Arcadian costume and as a shepherdess – she holds a shepherdess's staff. There are numerous Dutch portraits of the period of men and women as shepherds and shepherdesses; and it is probable that the twenty-nine-year-old Rembrandt, recently married and recently settled in Amsterdam, where such pictures became popular in the early 1630s, was here following a contemporary fashion. Whether she is *Flora*, a shepherdess, or just Saskia, the picture has a joyfulness and delicate beauty unique among the portraits by Rembrandt in the National Gallery.

See colour plate page 113

HENDRICK TER BRUGGHEN (?1588–1629)
A Man playing a Lute
100.5 × 78.7 cm
Signed: *H T Brugghen . fecit . 1624* (HTB in monogram)

Ter Brugghen was one of several Dutch painters who went to Rome in the early years of the seventeenth century and was there influenced by the lighting effects and in his choice of subject-matter by Caravaggio (d. 1610) and his Roman followers. He returned to Utrecht about 1615. From about 1620 he painted several pictures of single musicians in fancy dress. These figures, painted against a blank background, often make a direct appeal to the spectator, and the attractiveness of the pictures is enhanced by the exceptional beauty of the painting and the clarity of the colouring.

GABRIEL METSU (1629–67)
A Man and Woman beside a Virginal
38.4 × 32.2 cm
Signed: *G. Metsu*

As in many Dutch seventeenth-century genre pictures the scene here is one of courtship, to which music is a traditional and obvious accompaniment. It is perhaps with irony that the virginal (which appears also in other paintings by the artist) is inscribed with verses from the Psalms: 'In thee Lord do I put my trust, let me never be ashamed.' The picture on the back wall (left) is a known painting by Metsu (now in the Alte Pinakothek, Munich) and shows the *Twelfth Night Feast*. The boisterous nature of the feast is no doubt intended to contrast with the dignified exchange between the couple in the foreground.

AELBERT CUYP (1620–91)
A Hilly River Landscape
135.2 × 200 cm
Signed: *A: cuyp*

A mounted horseman in a brilliant red coat has stopped to ask the way of a shepherdess tending her sheep. Like the birds wheeling their way across the sky to roost, he too seems to be towards the end of his travels, while cattle and sheep also lie down to rest.

The picture is painted from a low viewpoint which emphasizes the contours of the foreground details of dogs, cattle – even weeds and grasses. The light, strong only in the very foreground where it highlights the foliage, permeates the landscape and imbues it with a warm evening glow. A darkly coloured foreground becomes light as it reaches the horizon

and detail is diffused into yellow shadowy forms.

Cuyp was born in Dordrecht, where he passed all his life, and possibly only rarely left the city. Yet it is hard to believe that his intensely poetic vision of landscape could have been inspired by that of his native Holland. He never went to Italy, but his pictures share the same mood as those by Claude Lorraine which were inspired by the Roman Campagna. Other Dutch painters of his time did travel to Italy and returned, mainly to Utrecht, bringing with them an Italianate style in painting. It was they, in particular Jan Both, who influenced Cuyp; but he surpassed all of them in his mastery of light.

Of all Dutch landscape painters Cuyp has always been the most popular with British collectors, and like Claude, who was also much collected, his paintings had enormous influence on later British landscape painters.

MEYNDERT HOBBEMA (1638–1709)
The Avenue, Middelharnis
103.5 × 141 cm
Signed: *M: hobbema f 1689*

Middelharnis is a village on the north coast of the island of Over Flakee in the mouth of the Maas in the province of South Holland. Hobbema's picture was painted in 1689, twenty-five years after the trees along the avenue were planted. The view is still recognizable, although the trees are gone and the church of Middelharnis, to the left of the avenue, has lost its bulbous spire.

The picture is a masterpiece of breathtaking simplicity. The severely foreshortened avenue directs the attention of the spectator to the distant view of the small village protruding above the flat horizon. From the distance figures walk towards the spectator along the avenue, thereby emphasizing its indefinite distance, while spindly trees sway against a cold and cloudy sky.

Hobbema was a pupil in Amsterdam of Jacob van Ruisdael – perhaps the greatest of all Dutch landscape painters. Some of his pictures approximate very strongly to those of his teacher; but in a picture such as *The Avenue, Middelharnis*, one of the last great Dutch landscapes, Ruisdael's more romantic, stormy nature gives way to peaceful understatement.

PHILIPS KONINCK (1619–88)
An Extensive Landscape with a Road by a Ruin
137.4 × 167.7 cm
Signed: *P. Koninck 1655*

According to a seventeenth-century biographer, Philips Koninck was a pupil of Rembrandt in Amsterdam; but this is now thought
to be unlikely. He was the son of a wealthy
goldsmith, and himself the well-to-do owner
of a shipping and hostelry business. In his lifetime he was known as a painter of portraits
and genre and history pictures; but today he is
best remembered for his panoramic views of
the flat Dutch countryside. In these, which are
generally painted from a high viewpoint, heavy
clouds seem to move across the landscape
allowing light through here and creating
shadows there.

JAN VAN GOYEN (1596–1656)
River Scene with Shipping
49.2 × 68.9 cm

Jan van Goyen, who worked from 1632 at The
Hague, was the most important Dutch landscape painter of the first half of the seventeenth
century. Many of his pictures are painted in
near monochrome, and he concentrated more
on achieving atmospheric effects than on
topographical delineation. Most of his works
contain water, but the chief glory of many of
them is the superb skies, which, as he employed
a low horizon, generally occupy about two-
thirds of the picture's space. As in the present
picture, the sky is often pierced by the
protruding forms of ships' sails or windmills,
and the tonal effect is set off by dark foreground figures.

PIETER DE HOOGH (1629–after 1684?)
The Courtyard of a House in Delft
73.5 × 60 cm
Signed: *P.D.H. AN° 1658*

De Hoogh worked in Delft in the 1650s and it was there, before his move to Amsterdam in the early 1660s, that he painted his best work. A contemporary in Delft was Vermeer, and their work has much in common: both were fascinated by the effects of falling light, and both painted scenes in which a doorway leads 'into' the picture towards a bright background. This picture is one of the earliest dated works by the artist.

Jacob van Ruisdael (*c.* 1628–82)
A Landscape with a ruined Castle and a Church
109.2 × 146.1 cm
Signed: *JvRuisdael* (*JvR* in monogram)

Jacob van Ruisdael was the greatest of all Dutch landscape painters. He had many imitators, and among his pupils was Hobbema, whose masterpiece, *The Avenue, Middelharnis*, is in the National Gallery. Ruisdael was born in Haarlem, the centre of a school of landscape painters in the early seventeenth century, and the artist's earliest pictures show the neighbourhood of his birthplace. In 1657 he moved to Amsterdam, where he lived until his death. In his last years he was less active as a painter and possibly practised as a surgeon – he is presumed to have taken a medical degree at Caen University in 1676.

This picture was probably painted some time in the late 1660s. The view is imaginary, but nevertheless one which the artist repeated in at least four other pictures, one of which is also in the National Gallery. The picture is typical of the painter's late work, being a panoramic view across a vast expanse of flat landscape. Here it is early morning and the day's first light breaks through the clouds and steals across the landscape. This treatment of light gives the picture a romantic quality, which was to appear in other of Ruisdael's paintings featuring waterfalls and pine trees. These latter pictures were inspired by the landscapes of Allart van Everdingen, who had visited Scandinavia.

On occasion, other artists painted the figures in Ruisdael's landscapes, and those in the left foreground of this painting, as well as the animals, are by Adriaen van de Velde, a painter who worked in Amsterdam and who often painted the figures and animals in the pictures of other artists.

CAREL FABRITIUS (1622–54)
Self-Portrait (?)
70.5 × 61.6 cm
Signed: *C. fabritius. 1654*

The informality and experimental nature of the picture, and the stare of the sitter towards the spectator, suggest that this painting is a self-portrait which would have been painted from a mirror; but as there is no extant documented likeness of Carel Fabritius one cannot be certain.

Fabritius, who worked in Delft, was a talented artist, a pupil of Rembrandt and an important influence on later Delft painters, such as De Hoogh and Vermeer. He produced little, however, because at the age of thirty-two he was killed in the explosion of the municipal arsenal at Delft which destroyed a large part of the city. This portrait was painted within months of his death.

FRANS HALS (?c. 1580–1666)
A Family Group in a Landscape
148.5 × 251 cm

The particular family in this elaborate picture remain unidentified. With the exception of the elderly lady, in old-fashioned clothes, they are dressed in the costume of the late 1640s. They are presumably husband and wife with their six children, a nurse or aunt and a grandmother.

In spite of the unnaturalness of their setting, all the people in the portrait have a spontaneity and liveliness, and as often with a modern-day photograph, the image seems to have been captured before all the sitters were quite prepared. After Rembrandt, whose style is quite different, Hals was the greatest Dutch portraitist of the seventeenth century, and his real genius was for group portraiture. Although he painted predominantly in tones of black and grey, with the paint often applied very broadly, his portraits have a marvellous liveliness on account of the virtuosity of his technique.

Although born in Antwerp, he worked most of his life in Haarlem, where he was enormously popular. In spite of this his pictures were largely unknown in the eighteenth century and were only 're-discovered' in the nineteenth, when his work influenced such painters as Manet and the Impressionists.

THOMAS DE KEYSER (1596/7–1667)
Constantijn Huygens and his (?) Clerk
92.4 × 69.3 cm
Signed: *TDK AN 1627* (*TDK* in monogram)

JOHANNES VERMEER (1632–75)
A Young Woman standing at a Virginal
52.7 × 45.2 cm
Signed: *IV Meer* (or *IMeer*; the capitals are in monogram)

Constantijn Huygens (1596–1687), after serving at the Dutch Embassy in London, where he was knighted by James I, was secretary to the Stadholders Prince Frederick Henry and later Willem II in Amsterdam. He was particularly interested in the fine arts and is shown in this portrait with architectural drawings, compasses and a *chittarone*, and globes, reflecting his interest in music, architecture and astronomy. The tapestry in the background, which shows St Francis before the Sultan, is woven with Constantijn Huygens's coat of arms in the upper border.

The painting on the back wall of the room in which the lady is playing the virginal alludes to the subject-matter of Vermeer's picture. It shows a cupid holding a playing card aloft, a

Perfectus Amor non est nisi ad unum, from
Amorum Emblemata by Otto Vaenius (1608)

gesture whose meaning is explained by one of the illustrations in Otto Vaenius's *Amorum Emblemata* (Antwerp, 1608). There Cupid holds a small tablet inscribed with the number 1 while he tramples on another inscribed with the numbers 2 to 10. The verse accompanying this illustration praises fidelity to one as opposed to the love of many. Vermeer's painting is therefore probably intended to represent a faithful woman.

Vermeer, who was forgotten until the late nineteenth century, worked in Delft and of all Dutch painters he was the greatest master at conveying the effects of falling light. His meticulous pictures (of which there are perhaps no more than forty in existence) are painted with a brilliant sense of colour. Many of his pictures, while apparently representing no more than a relatively simple Dutch interior, are generally symbolic in content.

SEBASTIANO RICCI (1659–1734)
Bacchus and Ariadne
75.9 × 63.2 cm

Ariadne, having been abandoned by Theseus on the island of Naxos, was discovered there while asleep by the god Bacchus on his return from the East: hence the leopards which accompany him in this painting. Bacchus, who brought in his train bacchantes, one with a tambourine, the other with cymbals, and a satyr and pipe-playing cherub, instantly fell in love with her and proposed marriage. In the sky *putti* carry a hymeneal torch (or marriage flame), thus celebrating the union of Bacchus and Ariadne.

The composition of the picture, which was probably painted in the first decade of the eighteenth century, is derived from a painting by a seventeenth-century Venetian painter, Giulio Carpione. It was not unusual for Ricci to copy the work of earlier painters and his 'discovery' of Veronese as a rich source of pictorial inspiration was enormously influential for the later development of eighteenth-century Venetian decorative painting.

Ricci, who was born north of Venice, travelled and worked as a young man outside of Italy; he came to England in 1712 when he hoped to be given the job of decorating the dome of St Paul's Cathedral. About 1716 he settled in Venice where he died in 1734.

GIOVANNI BATTISTA TIEPOLO (1696–1770)
A Vision of the Trinity to Pope St Clement(?)
69.2 × 55.2 cm

The picture is a *modello* for an altarpiece, once at Schloss Nymphenburg near Munich, and now in the Alte Pinakothek at Munich. A *modello* is a small-scale version of a large picture, generally executed by an artist in order to show a patron how the completed picture will look.

The design of this *modello* is of a familiar type and shows a kneeling saint receiving a vision of the Trinity. The saint is recognizable as a pope, for a seated angel near him holds a papal tiara and three-barred patriarchal papal cross; the vision is shown taking place inside a church;

the statue, top left, is of Faith. As the altarpiece was either commissioned or bought from Tiepolo by Clemens August, Archbishop-Elector of Cologne, the saint may be identified as the Archbishop-Elector's namesake, the second-century Pope, St Clement. Clemens August himself had visited Venice and had also commissioned altarpieces from two other Venetian artists, Pittoni and Piazzetta. The chapel at Nymphenburg, in which this altarpiece was installed, was consecrated in 1739 and it is likely that Tiepolo's painting was executed shortly before that.

Tiepolo was popular as a painter of altarpieces; several *modelli* like the present picture survive, including one other in the National Gallery.

GIOVANNI BATTISTA TIEPOLO (1696–1770)
The Banquet of Cleopatra
44.2 × 65.7 cm

The subject of the picture is the banquet given at Alexandria by Cleopatra for her lover the Roman statesman, Mark Antony. Cleopatra

Study by G.B. Tiepolo for *The Banquet of Cleopatra*
(Victoria & Albert Museum)

wagered Antony that she would spend a fortune on a single banquet. This she did, by dissolving one of her pearls, the largest and finest ever known, in a goblet of vinegar. The story is derived from Pliny's *Natural History*, which describes the properties of pearls.

The picture, which is a sketch, is one of the several treatments of the theme by Tiepolo, the most famous of which is an enormous fresco painted in the Palazzo Labia, Venice, some time in the 1740s.

The sketch, in contrast to the Palazzo Labia fresco, is horizontal in shape but nevertheless it may represent a preliminary idea for the subject by Tiepolo. A drawing of the subject by Tiepolo, which is related to the present picture, is in the Victoria and Albert Museum. The drawing is also linked with another National Gallery picture, which was among the most famous pictures in eighteenth-century Venice, Veronese's *Family of Darius before Alexander* (page 61). Tiepolo's background architecture and the standing page on the right are derived from Veronese.

G.B. TIEPOLO
*An Allegory with
Venus and Time*
See page 130

GIOVANNI BATTISTA TIEPOLO (1696–1770)
An Allegory with Venus and Time
292 × 190 cm

When Giovanni Domenico Tiepolo (Giovanni Battista's son) made an etching after the present picture he called it '*Il Parto di Venere*' ('*The Confinement of Venus*'). The painting indeed represents Venus, recognizable by her attributes of doves and chariot, while her son, Cupid, holding a quiver of arrows, flutters at the bottom of the composition. The baby boy to whom Venus has given birth is possibly Aeneas, and by consigning him to the arms of winged Time, the goddess suggests that he may be immortal because as Time's scythe has fallen he probably represents Eternity. In what is possibly a preliminary drawing for the picture, Venus half-embraces Time, who nurses the new-born child. The Three Graces are in attendance on a cloud and prepare to shower the new-born boy with roses.

The picture, which was once part of a ceiling decoration in a palace of the Contarini family in Venice, may well have been commissioned by a member of the family to celebrate the birth of an heir. The family may have hoped for their heir to have the attributes, valour and strength of the Trojan hero. If neither of these possibilities occurred to them, then in a general way they certainly could have considered their son to be born of Beauty; and as he is consigned to Eternity, his future, and that of the Contarini family, seem assured.

The Venetian G. B. Tiepolo was the greatest decorative painter of the eighteenth century. This picture was probably painted in the 1750s when the artist was at the height of his fame. He was chiefly patronized by the Venetian aristocracy, but he also carried out frescoed decorations at Würzburg and, for the Spanish royal family, in Madrid, where he died.

See colour plate page 129

Venus giving Cupid to Time by G. B. Tiepolo
(Metropolitan Museum, New York)

GIOVANNI DOMENICO TIEPOLO (1727–1804)
*The Marriage of Frederick Barbarossa and
Beatrice of Burgundy*
72.4 × 52.6 cm

The Emperor Frederick I of Germany and
Beatrice of Burgundy were married at Würzburg in 1156 by the Prince-Bishop of Würzburg, Gebbhard von Henneberg. Six centuries
later, in 1749, the then Prince-Bishop, Carl
Phillipp von Greiffenclau, commissioned Giovanni Domenico's father G.B. Tiepolo, to
decorate the staircase and Kaisersaal of his
palace with frescoes which include that event.
This picture seems to be a record of the fresco,
though there are some differences between the
two. Drawings at Stuttgart, which may be
preparatory drawings by G.B. Tiepolo for the

Details of drawings by G.B. Tiepolo for
the frescoes in the Residenz at Würzburg
(Staatsgalerie, Stuttgart)

fresco, show the page holding the train and the
crown on the cushion. Tiepolo, influenced
throughout his life by the work of the
sixteenth-century Venetian painter Veronese,
characteristically places the marriage in a
setting more reminiscent of sixteenth-century
Venice than twelfth-century Germany.

CANALETTO (1697–1768)
Venice: the Basin of S. Marco on Ascension Day
121.9 × 182.8 cm

The view is towards the Doge's Palace with the campanile of S. Marco rising behind. To the left is the domed church of S. Maria della Salute. The picture records the embarkation of the Doge for the annual Ascension Day ceremony of the Wedding of the Sea. Canaletto painted several versions of the subject.

The custom of the Doge being rowed in state to the mouth of the Lido on Ascension Day originally commemorated a Venetian naval victory in the tenth century. Then in 1178 Pope Alexander III presented the Doge with a ring, in gratitude for having saved the Papacy from Frederick Barbarossa. On subsequent Ascension Day ceremonies the Doge would bless a ring and throw it into the water. When Canaletto painted his picture, the ceremony was an anachronism for by the eighteenth century Venice's power, both at sea and on the mainland, had long since declined. The Wedding of the Sea served only as a nostalgic reminder of her days of former grandeur.

CANALETTO (1697–1768)
Venice: Campo S. Vidal and S. Maria della Carità
('*The Stonemason's Yard*')
123.8 × 162.9 cm

The view is from the Campo S. Vidal across the Grand Canal to S. Maria della Carità. The campanile of S. Maria della Carità collapsed in 1744, but apart from that the view which Canaletto painted remains largely unchanged and the stone well-head is still there. The picture has long been affectionately known as *The Stonemason's Yard*, but there is no history of there ever having been a stonemason's yard at the Campo S. Vidal, and Canaletto did not usually paint *capricci* (imaginary views). The church of S. Vidal was rebuilt in the early years of the eighteenth century, and these stonemason's huts and half-hewn stone blocks are likely to be connected with that project. The picture, probably painted about 1730, is an early painting by the artist, and a masterpiece.

What is possibly the key to the painting's attraction is that it is not a usual view. The other paintings by Canaletto in the National Gallery (and indeed most other paintings by Canaletto) show the tourist's Venice: regattas on the Grand Canal, the Ascension Day ceremony of the Wedding of the Sea, and the Piazza S. Marco. But in *The Stonemason's Yard* the spectacle is simply that of everyday life: a woman draws water from a well, another hangs out bed-clothes and her neighbour pauses in her sweeping to tend a crying child.

Before Canaletto other painters, notably Luca Carlevaris (1665–1731), had executed views of Venice; but it was Canaletto who developed the genre, and he had many followers. Venice in the eighteenth century was one of the most visited of all European cities; and it was for the tourist market that Canaletto's views were exclusively painted. It is hardly surprising, therefore, that such scenes as *The Stonemason's Yard* are relatively rare in his œuvre, for few English milords would want such scenes of Venetian everyday life.

FRANCESCO GUARDI (1712–93)
Venice: The Punta della Dogana with S. Maria della Salute
56.2 × 75.9 cm

There are several paintings by Guardi which show this same view. Like Canaletto, Guardi painted his views of Venice from nature, from engravings after other artists' work, or from memory. This view is based on a drawing by Guardi (now in the Albertina, Vienna) – and whereas sometimes the artist's finished pictures differ considerably from his drawings, this one is closely related to it, and many details such as the sails of the boats and the poses of the gondoliers are identical.

As a young man, Guardi may have worked with Canaletto; but his views of Venice are much more atmospheric than those of the earlier master and as such they perhaps appeal to us more today.

The Punta della Dogana by Guardi
(Albertina, Vienna)

PIETRO LONGHI (1702?–85)
Exhibition of a Rhinoceros at Venice
60.4 × 47 cm

Brought to Europe in 1741 by Captain David Montvandermeer, the rhinoceros was probably the first seen by Europeans for over two centuries. It was therefore a celebrated animal: a learned scholar, Scipione Maffei, published a dissertation on it in 1751, and it 'sat' for its portrait several times and in several places, including Paris, where Oudry painted it in 1750.

Longhi was commissioned by at least two patrons to paint it when it came to Venice for the Carnival of 1751; and this picture is inscribed on the back of the canvas, *per commissione del Nobile Uomo Sier Girolamo Mocenizo Patrizio Veneto*. Most of Longhi's naïve little pictures of patrician Venetians are known in several versions and, as in the case of the present painting, he himself painted replicas. He also had imitators and pupils who duplicated his designs further. His style is often compared with that of his English con-

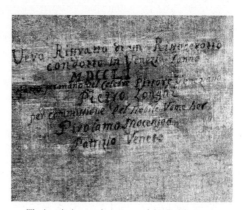

The inscription on the reverse of the *Exhibition of a Rhinoceros at Venice* by Longhi which records that the picture was painted for Girolamo Mocenigo

temporary, Hogarth: both painted scenes of daily life. But there the comparison ends, for Hogarth saw fit to satirize that life and point to its foibles in a manner which would have been quite alien to Longhi.

JEAN-BAPTISTE CHARDIN (1699–1779)
The Young Schoolmistress
61.6 × 66.7 cm
Signed: *chardin*

Chardin's subject-matter is generally not much different from that of some Dutch seventeenth-century painters: still-life and everyday scenes of bourgeois life. But the application of his paint and the superbly delicate sense of colour are very different. Furthermore, Chardin's paintings generally contain a moral, often on a theme of discipline or the benefits of education. Here a young child is firmly made to concentrate by his young teacher who may well be his sister.

JEAN-BAPTISTE PERRONNEAU (1715?–83)
Portrait of Jacques Cazotte
89 × 71.5 cm
Signed: *Perroneau*

This delightfully informal, witty and very French portrait is of Jacques Cazotte (1719–92), a poet and novelist who was guillotined during the French Revolution. Perronneau was best known as a pastellist. This painting is in oil but it has much of the delicacy associated with the chalkiness of the pastellist's medium.

NICOLAS LANCRET (1690–1743)
A Lady and a Gentleman with two Girls in a Garden ('La Tasse de chocolat')
88.9 × 97.8 cm

As a family portrait (the family have not been identified) this picture has a charm that raises it above the type of fête-galante (derived from Watteau) which Lancret usually painted. It was exhibited, as a lady 'prenant du Caffe avec des enfants', at the Salon of 1742, the last of Lancret's lifetime.

Study by Goya for a portrait of the
Duke of Wellington. (British Museum)

FRANCISCO DE GOYA (1746–1828)
The Duke of Wellington
64.3 × 52.4 cm

As general in command of British forces in
Spain during the Peninsular War, the first
Duke of Wellington (1769–1852) defeated
Napoleon's brother Joseph, King of Spain, at
the Battle of Vitoria in 1813. After the Battle of
Salamanca Wellington entered Madrid on
12 August 1812 and left it on 1 September.
While he was there Goya painted (on a
mahogany panel) this portrait, but made
alterations to it subsequently.

The first state of the portrait probably
corresponded to a drawing of the Duke by
Goya now in the British Museum. In that
Wellington wears a plain jacket, the Peninsular
Medallion on a ribbon about his neck and three
stars on his chest. But the liveliness of the
painted portrait suggests that the drawing was

done merely to establish the pose, and the
painting done from life. On subsequent occasions, possibly in May 1814 when the Duke
paid a second visit to Madrid, Goya altered
the Duke's uniform: it is now unrecognizable
as any known British military dress. He also
added the pink sash, the Order of the Golden
Fleece, the Gold Cross and other decorations.

In the portrait as we now see it the Duke
wears the Order of the Golden Fleece (awarded
him in August 1812) on a red ribbon about his
neck; the Military Gold Cross surmounted by
three clasps; the Order of the Bath (top); the
Portuguese Order of the Tower and Sword
(lower left); and the Spanish Order of San
Fernando (lower right). Two other paintings
of the Duke of Wellington by Goya are known:
an equestrian portrait (now in Apsley House,
London) in which the features of the Duke are
superimposed on those of an earlier sitter, and
a half-length portrait now in the National
Gallery, Washington.

GEORGE STUBBS (1724–1806)
The Milbanke and Melbourne Families
97 × 149 cm

The sitters are traditionally identified as, from left to right, Lady Melbourne, *née* Elizabeth Milbanke (1751–1818), her father Sir Ralph Milbanke (1722–98), her brother John Milbanke (d. 1800) and her husband the first Viscount Melbourne (1748–1828). The picture was probably painted about 1770. Sir Ralph Milbanke was the grandfather of Anne Isabella Milbanke, who married the poet Lord Byron.

During the second half of the eighteenth century 'country life' became the passion of the English upper classes. Country-house building reached its peak and among the new landed aristocracy hunting and racing developed in popularity. This was the class that patronized Stubbs, and his genius has left for us an image of the age that is supreme. *The Milbanke and Melbourne Families* is in the tradition of a conversation piece: miniature portraits in their natural setting. It is an intensely English picture: the spreading tree, the foxgloves and the cool mist over the lake in the background is the natural setting for this typical upper-class family—a rather dowdy daughter who has married well, her sensible father, her coxcomb brother and her dutiful husband.

Stubbs was born in Liverpool and first worked as a portraitist. He is chiefly known for his paintings of horses, a subject which fascinated him. His *Anatomy of the Horse*, published in 1767, is a work of scientific research based on drawings made from the dissected carcasses of horses.

SIR JOSHUA REYNOLDS (1723–92)
General Sir Banastre Tarleton
236.2 × 145.4 cm

The sitter, who was twenty-eight when the portrait was painted, distinguished himself on the British side during the American War of Independence. After fighting in North Carolina he returned to England, a popular hero, early in 1782. Almost immediately he was painted by both Reynolds and Gainsborough (the latter portrait now lost) and both portraits were exhibited at the Royal Academy that year. Later in life Tarleton achieved notoriety by becoming the lover of Mrs Robinson ('Perdita') and so cuckolding the Prince of Wales. In the portrait Reynolds discreetly indicates that Tarleton had lost two fingers from his right hand. He wears the green uniform of Tarleton's Green Horse, a cavalry branch of the troop known as the British Legion which was raised by him during the American War of Independence. The flag bears an eagle, cannon and a wreathed 'L'.

Reynolds, dissatisfied that British patrons in the eighteenth century collected only Old

The Lansdowne House Hermes by a Greek sculptor of the fourth century BC. Photograph here printed in reverse. (Ny Carlsberg Glyptotek, Copenhagen)

Masters and commissioned nothing but portraits from British painters, attempted throughout his career to raise the standard and status of British art. This he did often by depicting his sitters in poses derived from Old Masters or Antique sculpture and, going a step further, clothed in 'classical' costumes. His more extreme essays in this manner can now appear unsympathetic; but a portrait such as that of Banastre Tarleton succeeds brilliantly because the pose (which is probably inspired by a statue of *Hermes* dating from the fourth century BC) seems quite natural and without affectation. It is perfectly reasonable that Tarleton should pause to adjust his leggings on the battlefield and that the horses should be frenzied at the sounds of firing cannon. The *Hermes*, imported into England in the 1770s, shortly before Reynolds painted this picture, was at Lansdowne House, London, and was one of the most celebrated statues of the day.

SIR JOSHUA REYNOLDS (1723–92)
Lord Heathfield
142.2 × 113.7 cm

The sitter is George Augustus Eliott (1717–90), created Lord Heathfield in 1787. He was a Scotsman, educated at the University of Leyden and later at the French military college, La Fère. One-time aide-de-camp to George II, he was a distinguished soldier, and in 1775 was appointed Governor of Gibraltar when a Spanish invasion of the Rock seemed imminent. From 1775 to 1783 he successfully withstood the Spanish siege and upon his return to England was created a Knight of the Bath, whose Ribbon and Star he is wearing in the portrait, and Lord Heathfield.

The picture was commissioned from Reynolds by Alderman John Boydell, a famous print publisher, for after Heathfield had become a popular hero there would have been a lively demand for engraved portraits of him. He sat to Reynolds in August and September 1787. The artist chose a pose which made him look for all the world like an eighteenth-century St Peter, holding in his hand the key, not to the Kingdom of Heaven, but merely to that of Gibraltar. Behind him the smoke of warfare rises and cannons are aimed at the shore below the Rock.

This is a very late picture by the artist and is a masterpiece. In it Reynolds has discarded his rigid application of what he thought of as the Grand Style. Lord Heathfield is not, as one might expect him to be, depicted in the armour of some Roman general; instead the pose is relatively informal, and therein lies the power of the portrait.

THOMAS GAINSBOROUGH (1727–88)
The Morning Walk
236.2 × 179.1 cm

The sitters are William Hallett (1764–1842) and his wife Elizabeth, *née* Stephen (1763/4–1833), who had been married on 30 July 1785. The picture was probably painted soon afterwards, as it was described in the *Morning Herald* of 30 March 1786 as having '*promenaded* from Gainsborough's gallery where it was no longer on view'. The title *The Morning Walk* is probably no older than the late nineteenth century.

Both Mr and Mrs Hallett are twenty-one, and as neither of them were famous, aristocratic or rich it is easy to see the picture as a simple portrait of young love. They do not look at each other, but communicate by the gentle touch of Mrs Hallett's hand on the arm of her husband. Their gazes are tinged with sadness—sadness that their present transports of shared happiness may not last, and the bond between them excludes all others: even the dog must await some attention in vain.

It is probable that the portrait was always interpreted in such terms, and indeed the Victorians invented a tragic end to the story. *The Critic* of 1859 gives the totally untrue information that Mrs Hallett died soon after the marriage, while Mr Hallett 'became a low debauched gambling roué, gouty, bloated, and poverty stricken, and married again some low person'.

143

become ill for the first time – he was later declared to be insane, and the Queen personally undertook to look after him. Sittings for the portrait were difficult, but in spite of that the picture is a triumph. The painter who was just twenty at the time did not care for the dress chosen by the Queen, and when he asked her to converse with her daughters, the Princesses, 'to give animation to the countenance . . . her Majesty thought that rather presuming, and continued to listen to one of them reading'. The Queen then refused a final sitting; and it was Mrs Papendiek who modelled the positions of the bracelets and scarf.

THOMAS GAINSBOROUGH (1727–88)
Mr and Mrs Andrews
69.8 × 119 cm

The sitters are traditionally identified as Robert Andrews (?1726–1806) and his wife Frances Mary, *née* Carter (*c.* 1723–80). They were married in 1748, about four years before Gainsborough painted their portrait. They are painted on their farm Auberies near Sudbury in Suffolk. The church in the background (centre) is St Peter's, Sudbury and the tower to the left is that of Lavenham church.

It was unusual, if not exceptional, for Gainsborough to paint an identifiable view, but the spot where Mr and Mrs Andrews are shown seated is still recognizable today. The tree is still there and the land is still arable, although planting now obscures the distant views. Although the figures in the picture are almost doll-like (Gainsborough in fact made figure studies from dressed-up dolls), the artist seems intent on showing Mr Andrews as a farmer. The corn is well harvested, the distant fields are enclosed with hedges and well-painted gates, and cattle to the left are sheltered by sheds. Mr Andrews carries a gun, for by eighteenth-century game laws only those qualified by estate or social standing might shoot game. The picture therefore reflects an interest in agriculture, which at the time was a relatively new 'enthusiasm' for the English upper and middle classes.

Gainsborough was in his late twenties when he painted the picture. He had by then returned to his native Suffolk after an apprenticeship, possibly to a French engraver, Hubert Gravelot, in London. Elements of the picture, such as the exquisite seat, are demonstrably Rococo,

SIR THOMAS LAWRENCE (1769–1830)
Queen Charlotte
239.4 × 147.3 cm

Charlotte Sophia of Mecklenburg-Strelitz married King George III in 1761 and was crowned Queen in that year. Horace Walpole described her as 'not tall nor a beauty. Pale and very thin; but looks sensible and genteel.' The picture was painted at Windsor and the view in the background is towards Eton College Chapel. The Queen wears a bracelet with a miniature of George III. The picture was probably painted in 1789 and exhibited at the Royal Academy the following year.

The circumstances under which the portrait was painted are described in the *Journals* of Mrs Papendiek who was 'Assistant Keeper of the Wardrobe and Reader to her Majesty'. When the artist was first introduced to the Queen 'her Majesty was rather averse to sitting to him, saying that she had not recovered sufficiently from all the trouble and anxiety she had gone through to give so young an artist a fair chance'. In the previous year the King had

reflecting the influence of Gravelot and other London-based French artists of the 1740s.

WILLIAM HOGARTH (1697–1764)
The Shrimp Girl
63.5 × 50.8 cm

A young Cockney fishwoman carries a platter of shrimps on her head. The picture is obviously unfinished, and clearly painted for the artist's pleasure: it remained in the possession of his widow until 1790. Mrs Hogarth called it '*The Market Wench*' and told those who looked at it: 'They say he could not paint flesh. There's flesh and blood for you; – them!'

Hogarth himself had written: 'When a subject is trifling or dull the execution must be excellent or the picture is nothing. If a subject is good providing such material parts are taken care of as may convey perfectly the sense, the action and the passion may be more truly and distinctly conveyed by a coarse, bold stroke than the most delicate finishing.' Certainly the artist must have felt that in *The Shrimp Girl* he had a good subject; the nose and mouth seem the only areas which are fully finished, and yet the portrait has a tremendous liveliness.

Hogarth is perhaps best known for his series of engravings, such as *Marriage à la Mode*; but it is in the presence of an uncontrived masterpiece like *The Shrimp Girl* that one realizes that he was a pure painter of outstanding genius.

WILLIAM HOGARTH (1697–1764)
A series: *Marriage à la Mode*
Each picture about 70 × 90.8 cm

These are the original six paintings from which engravings were made and published in 1745 to form perhaps the most famous of all Hogarth's moral series. The subject of the series is contemporary high life and a marriage based on money and vanity.

The Marriage Contract
The engaged couple, soon to be fettered like the pair of dogs in front of them, are on the left. They express little interest in each other, indeed the girl's attention is entirely taken up by Counsellor Silvertongue, the lawyer who is soon to become her lover. To the right the father of the girl, a wealthy alderman and the young Viscount's father, the gouty Lord Squander, negotiate the contract. Lord Squander indicates that his family tree may be traced back to William the Conqueror.

Shortly after the Marriage
The disarray of the room is evidence that the marriage is also in disarray, and the painting over the chimneypiece shows Cupid ironically commenting on the loveless union by playing bagpipes. The young wife is breakfasting late after a card party, and the little dog discovers a woman's handkerchief in the pocket of the Viscount, who has just returned from a drunken night out.

The Visit to the Quack Doctor
The subject of this picture is venereal disease, and the Viscount jovially brings his mistress, who is scarcely more than a girl, to visit a quack doctor. The sinister nature of the subject is suggested by the objects in the room, while behind the couple, even the skeleton seems to be making amorous advances to its neighbour.

The Countess's Morning Levée
The heroine, now a countess, as shown by the coronets on her bed and mirror, gives a levée, but ignores all her guests except Silvertongue, who is inviting her to a masquerade. The progress of their intrigue is indicated by the Negro boy in the foreground who points to the horns of Actaeon. The pictures on the wall, apart from the portrait of Silvertongue, illustrate themes of licentiousness: *Jupiter and Io*, *The Rape of Ganymede*, *Lot and his daughters*. On the left an Italian castrato is singing, accompanied by a flautist.

The Killing of the Earl
The scene is a bagnio where the Countess and Silvertongue have gone after the masquerade. The Earl has surprised them, and Silvertongue, shown escaping through the window, has killed him.

The Suicide of the Countess
The Countess has just read on a broadsheet that Silvertongue has been hanged for killing her husband, the Earl. Her child by the Earl embraces her (he is shown to be, like his father, diseased), while her father removes a diamond ring from her finger. The room, which is intended to be in the house of the Countess's father, shows evidence of poverty – the broken window panes and the hungry dog. Perhaps her father is naturally mean, or more likely, he has spent all his money on his daughter's dowry, and the marriage which was based on such vanity is now ended in squalor.

JOHN CONSTABLE (1776–1837)
The Haywain
130 × 185 cm
Signed: *John Constable pinxt. London 1821*

The artist, the greatest of English landscape painters, came from East Bergholt in Suffolk, and it was from the Suffolk landscape that he drew his inspiration. The scene of *The Haywain* is on the River Stour at Flatford Mill, which was owned by the painter's father, and the house in the picture is that of a neighbour, Willy Lot: 'Willy Lot was born in this house and is said to have passed more than eighty years without having spent four whole days away from it.'

The picture was exhibited at the Royal Academy in 1821 when the painter was forty-five, and although he had been exhibiting for almost twenty years, his work was still very much unappreciated. *The Haywain* was seen at the Academy by the French painter Géricault and made a tremendous impression upon him; and when later (in 1824) it was exhibited at the Paris Salon it created a sensation. Constable himself was intrigued to think 'of the lovely valleys and peaceful farm-houses of Suffolk forming a scene of exhibition to amuse the gay and frivolous Parisians' but the French artists who were impressed included Delacroix, and Constable's paintings were to influence the later French landscape painters of the Barbizon School.

Constable was among the earliest of landscape painters who attempted to depict the transient effects of nature: light, clouds and rain. This he did in small rapid sketches where he also 'stated' his composition. These small oil-sketches were followed by other sketches of different parts of the picture, and finally the artist made a full-size study in oils of the final picture. In comparison with the full-size studies, the finished pictures are more coherent, both in composition and colour, and for that reason seem more 'classical'. But this would not always have been so, and when looking at Constable's *Haywain* it does well to remember that it was painted as early as 1821, more than fifty years before the Impressionists created the type of landscape of which it was a precursor, and which today we consider 'normal'.

J.M.W. TURNER (1775–1851)
Ulysses deriding Polyphemus
132 × 203 cm

The subject is taken from Homer's *Odyssey*, Pope's translation of which was probably used by Turner:

The land of Cyclops lay in prospect near. . .
And from their mountains rising smokes appear.

Polyphemus, a one-eyed Cyclops, imprisoned Ulysses with twelve of his companions in a cave. Turner's picture shows Ulysses, having blinded Polyphemus, escaping at dawn: the sun drawn by horses rises to the right. The shadowy figure of Polyphemus is seen above the ship of Ulysses, upon which sailors scramble to raise the sails, while the ship's swift passage is assisted by sea-nymphs.

John Ruskin, the artist's greatest champion, regarded this picture as 'the *central picture* in Turner's career' a view which is shared by most modern critics. He also considered 'the sky. . . [to be] . . . beyond comparison the finest that exists in Turner's oil paintings'. The picture was exhibited at the Royal Academy in 1829 and is based on a sketch which the artist almost certainly painted in Italy on his second visit there, in 1828/9. The particularly brilliant use of colour in the picture marks a departure from the artist's earlier paintings and opens the way for 'typical' late Turners. A contemporary critic considered the picture 'a specimen of *colouring run mad*'.

Although the subject of the picture is 'traditional' and drawn from mythology, Turner's treatment of it is 'modern' in that it reflects a preoccupation with the force and reality of nature. The mountain of Polyphemus, smoke billowing from it and fire below, is recognizably volcanic, and the phosphorescent sea-spray, cast up by the speed of Ulysses' ship, is suggested by the sea-nymphs.

JOHANN ZOFFANY (1733?–1810)
Mrs Oswald
226.5 × 158.8 cm

The identity of the sitter is not certain, but she is probably Mary Oswald, the daughter of Alexander Ramsey of Jamaica, who married Richard Oswald in 1750 and died in 1788. The costume indicates that the picture was probably painted in the first half of the 1760s. Zoffany was a German painter who worked in England from 1761. This portrait of a middle-aged woman in a landscape is a masterpiece of exquisite understatement.

JOHN CONSTABLE (1776–1837)
Salisbury Cathedral and Archdeacon Fisher's House
52.7 × 76.8 cm

Constable's friend Archdeacon Fisher had the use of the house known as Leydenhall in the Cathedral Close at Salisbury during his lifetime. In July and August 1820, Constable, his wife and two daughters stayed with the Fishers

at Leydenhall and it was almost certainly at that time that this picture was painted. The house is partly hidden by the trees on the right; in the background is the cathedral spire, and the river in the foreground is the Avon. The picture has all the appearances of a sketch painted from nature. On his return to London Constable wrote to the Archdeacon 'My Salisbury sketches are much liked – that in the Palace grounds – the bridges – and your house from the meadows.'

J.M.W. TURNER (1775–1851)
The 'Fighting Téméraire' tugged to her last Berth to be broken up, 1838
90.8 × 121.9 cm

The picture was exhibited at the Royal Academy of 1839 with the quotation in the catalogue: 'The flag which braved the battle and the breeze, no longer owns her.' The *Téméraire*, which took its name from a French ship which had been captured in 1759 at Lagos Bay, was a warship of ninety-eight guns that had been launched in 1798. Her crew distinguished themselves at the Battle of Trafalgar in 1805, after which the ship was known as *The Fighting Téméraire*. She was taken out of service in 1838, had her masts removed at Sheerness (where the temporary masts visible in Turner's picture were fitted) and on 18 September 1838 was towed from there by the Thames to Rotherhithe to be broken up. Turner very possibly saw that voyage. In his picture the ghostly form of the old ship is contrasted with the powerful black tug; and the poignancy of the *Téméraire*'s last voyage is emphasized by the brilliantly setting sun. The picture is about age, the age of the old ship contrasted with the youth of the tug, and symbolically suggesting the passing of an old era and the emergence of the new industrial one.

J.A.D. INGRES (1780–1867)
Madame Moitessier seated
120 × 92 cm
Signed: *J. Ingres 1856*

The sitter is Marie-Clotilde-Inès de Foucauld, who was born in 1821 and who married Sigisbert Moitessier in 1842. She died in 1897. When the artist was first asked to paint the portrait, shortly after her marriage, he refused, and only after being introduced to Madame Moitessier, and being struck by her beauty, did he agree to paint her.

Although not finally delivered until 1857, the portrait was started as early as 1844/5. At first it included, standing at her mother's knee, the sitter's small daughter Catherine, with Madame Moitessier's left hand resting on her head. Ingres, who at first thought Catherine 'charmante' later found her 'insupportable', and possibly for that reason erased her from the portrait. An alternative explanation would be that in the period over which the portrait was painted Catherine would have grown considerably, and as an almost grown-up girl might well have dominated a picture which was intended primarily to represent her mother. Probably about the time of the death of his wife

EUGÈNE DELACROIX (1798–1863)
Christ on the Cross
73.3 × 59.5 cm
Signed: *Eug. Delacroix 1853*

This is one of several paintings of the Crucifixion by Delacroix, who, in his later life, was attracted more and more towards painting religious subjects, particularly those related to Christ's Passion. With his own art constantly rejected by the public, Delacroix himself suffered much in later life and we know from his diaries that he was despondent during his last years. His treatment of the Crucifixion is a highly emotional one, with the swooning Maries at the foot of the Cross, the menacing sky and the strongly shadowed figure of the crucified Christ. This is a picture of suffering more human than religious. As it was painted in 1853, ten years before the artist's death, one may see it as a personal statement of his own torments.

Delacroix, the major painter of the Romantic movement in France, was inspired in his use of colour by Constable, Veronese and Rubens. An earlier treatment of *Christ on the Cross* by him is closely based on Rubens's famous picture of the same subject, the *Coup de Lance*.

Detail of a Roman fresco from Herculaneum depicting *Herakles and Telephus* (Museo Nazionale, Naples)

in 1849, Ingres abandoned the portrait, and it was only after the completion of another portrait of the same lady standing (now in the National Gallery, Washington), in 1851, that he resumed work on the present picture which was eventually finished in 1856. The pose is derived from an Antique painting from Herculaneum, now in the Museum at Naples, a copy of which Ingres possessed. The setting, with the large mirror reflecting a profile of the sitter's face, is typically ingenious.

Ingres was a superb draughtsman, and his strict classical style with his brilliant use of line and contour made him the direct opponent of the Romantic movement as expressed in the work of Delacroix. Madame Moitessier's fleshiness is contained within the supreme contours of her arms and shoulders. The chintz of her gown, her jewels and the furnishings of the room in which she is seated convey the wealth of someone of her social class in the period in which she lived, that of the Second Empire.

EUGÈNE DELACROIX (1798–1863)
Baron Schwiter
217.8 × 143.5 cm
Signed: *Euge Delacroix*

Baron Louis-Auguste Schwiter (1805–84) was twenty-one when this portrait was painted. He was a life-long friend of Delacroix and was named by the painter on his death as one of those who were to take charge of and classify his drawings. Delacroix also bequeathed him paintings by Watteau and Chardin. Schwiter himself was a reasonably successful painter, exhibiting landscapes and portraits at the Salon between 1831 and 1859. He was also a collector. Delacroix's treatment of the sitter is immensely sympathetic. Youthfully handsome, an aristocrat rather than an artist (he possibly wears a decoration below his waistcoat), Schwiter stands in the portrait constrained by the formality of his black clothes and fixing the spectator with an uneasy glance. There is a tradition that part of the landscape background in the portrait was painted by Paul Huet (1803–69), a painter who knew Delacroix through the latter's teacher P.N. Guérin.

Like many of the artist's pictures the *Portrait of Baron Schwiter* was refused (in 1827) by the Salon, for Delacroix's romantic style in painting was opposed to the classicism favoured in official Parisian art circles. The landscape with brooding, almost eerie, distant hills is romantic and Delacroix displays his powers as a colourist in the heavily impastoed flowers and the juxtaposition of the blue vase and red hat-lining. As an artist, Delacroix was the antithesis of his contemporary, the great draughtsman Ingres; in an area such as the sitter's right hand the form, rather than being drawn, is allowed to emerge subtly and beautifully from the paint.

PAUL DELAROCHE (1795–1856)
The Execution of Lady Jane Grey
246 × 297 cm

Lady Jane Grey (1537–54) had a distant claim to the throne of England as a great grand-daughter of Henry VII and upon the death of the young King, Edward VI, who was a Protestant like herself, she was proclaimed Queen and reigned for nine days in 1553. The party of the Roman Catholic Mary I, however, proved to be stronger, and Lady Jane was convicted of high treason, sentenced to death and executed in the Tower of London on 12 February 1554 at the age of seventeen. She was noted for her beauty and exceptional in-telligence and met her fate with pious and stoical resignation. This picture is a historical treatment of the subject of her execution, painted in the nineteenth century, when there was a vogue for historical subject-matter. It melodramatically emphasizes the tragic nature of the scene. Lady Jane's satin dress is as pure as she, and as yet unstained by blood. She is supported probably by the Lieutenant of the Tower, Sir John Brydges, while a lady-in-waiting, having removed Lady Jane's jewels, has fainted.

The picture created a sensation when exhibited at the Paris Salon in 1834 at a time when Delaroche was at the height of his popularity. Drawing his subject-matter from history, and frequently illustrating the tragic moments in the lives of famous men and women, Delaroche produced huge pictures which appealed to the Parisians, many of whom had witnessed similar scenes in the streets of their own city.

JEAN-BAPTISTE COROT (1796–1875)
The Roman Campagna, with the Claudian Aqueduct
21.6 × 33 cm
Signed: COROT

It is morning in the Roman Campagna and we are near the Via Appia Nuova looking towards the remains of the Aqua Claudia (the arches to right and left).

Many painters had been inspired by the Roman Campagna – among them another Frenchman, Claude Lorraine, in the seventeenth century. With Claude the Campagna was but inspiration; his great classical landscapes were rarely real views, but distillations of what the artist saw in the countryside round Rome. With Corot the view is real, and what is more the picture was painted on the spot directly from nature. Claude had imbued his landscapes with suggestive atmospheres, but Corot actually conveys the air (or lack of it) over the sun-baked fields, and it seems unlikely that the rain, promised by the clouds, will ever fall.

Datable about 1826, this is an early picture by the artist, who was born in Paris but travelled in Italy between 1825 and 1827. It was while painting out of doors in Italy that he developed his individual treatment of landscapes: broad areas of colour, little use of half tones and brilliantly strong cast shadows.

ÉDOUARD MANET (1832–83)
Music in the Tuileries Gardens
76 × 118 cm
Signed: *ed Manet 1862*

The scene is in the Tuileries gardens in Paris and the picture is dated 1862. A nineteenth-century account describes how Manet 'went almost every day to the Tuileries from two to four and made studies in the open air of children playing under the trees and groups of nurses slumped in chairs. Baudelaire was his constant companion.' In the picture the figure in profile against the large tree to the left is the poet Baudelaire, Manet's friend and champion. On the extreme left is the artist himself, and his brother Eugène is the person standing in profile right of centre. The man with the moustache, seated to the right against a tree is the composer Offenbach. The orchestra which

has attracted such a distinguished audience is not visible in the picture, nor indeed can it be said that the audience is giving the music their undivided attention.

Such an open-air scene suited the artist's technique. He used brilliant contrasts between light and shadow and painted with black to stupendous effect. In this picture the dappled sunshine which falls through the trees enhances the sense of animation in the scene. Some of the figures seem to be left unfinished; some, such as the two ladies in the foreground, are given undue prominence.

This is one of the earliest pictures in which Manet painted a bustling scene of fashionable contemporary life. Such paintings were either ridiculed or rejected by the Parisian art public and were constantly refused by the Salon. Manet, however, unlike some of his artist contemporaries, did not want to be a rebel, and longed for official acceptance.

CLAUDE MONET (1840–1926)
The Thames below Westminster
47 × 72.5 cm

CAMILLE PISSARRO (1830–1903)
Lower Norwood under Snow
35.3 × 45.7 cm

GUSTAVE COURBET (1819–77)
The Girls of the Seine Banks
96.5 × 131.1 cm

Probably in September 1870, Monet and Pissarro, who were then comparatively unknown painters, came to London as refugees from the war between their own country and Prussia. Another refugee was the Parisian art dealer, Durand-Ruel, who established a gallery in Bond Street, where both artists exhibited. Pissarro settled in the London suburb of Norwood, and although he and Monet returned to France in 1871 both artists made subsequent visits to this country. This view of the *Thames below Westminster* by Monet, and Pissarro's view of *Lower Norwood* in winter, were painted on that first visit; and both were exhibited at Durand-Ruel's gallery, which was the chief means of bringing the Impressionists' paintings to the English public's attention.

Courbet's painting of two prostitutes on the banks of the Seine is a composition sketch for the large picture of the same subject now in the Petit Palais, Paris. When the picture was exhibited at the Salon of 1857 it caused a public outrage. The Parisian public did not welcome the opportunity to view such scenes of contemporary life presented in the name of art.

CLAUDE MONET (1840–1926)
Water Lilies
200.7 × 426.7 cm
Stamped: *Claude Monet*

The subject is the water-garden at the artist's house in Giverney, mid-way between Paris and Le Havre. Monet had bought a house there in 1890 and by diverting a stream created a water-garden in which he planted lilies. This lily-pond provided the theme of several series of paintings during his last years. The present enormous picture was painted some time after 1916 when the artist had a specially large studio built to accommodate a series of huge canvasses, almost re-creations in paint of the pond itself. Monet presented nineteen other canvasses from this series to the French state in 1922, and they were installed in the Orangerie in Paris five years later.

Earlier in his life Monet had also painted series of pictures with similar subject-matter: first *Poplar Trees*, then *Haystacks*, later the façade of *Rouen Cathedral* and the *Thames*. In those pictures the artist developed his technique to become the leading Impressionist painter. Paint is applied in touches to convey the flickering and changing effect of light on a surface; outlines are hazy, and colour, even in areas of shadow, is in a high key. Monet's paintings of water lilies, shimmering pools of colour devoid of form, and painted forty years after the great decade of Impressionism, 1870–80, are the ultimate in the artist's pursuit of his ideals.

It was a painting by Monet, which had as its theme the play of light on water, that had given the Impressionist movement its name. Called *Impression, Sunrise*, it was exhibited in Paris in 1874, when a critic derisively seized upon its title to dub a style of painting (which is now seen as perhaps the most important of 'modern' art movements) Impressionism.

HENRI ROUSSEAU (1844–1910)
Tropical Storm with a Tiger ('Surpris')
129.8 × 161.9 cm
Signed: *Henri Rousseau 1891*

With its highly fanciful subject-matter, and meticulously painted very strong colours, the painting is typical of the artist's work. Although Rousseau (who is called le Douanier because he held a post in a toll station outside Paris) never had anything but the highest opinion of his own work, his genius was for long unrecognized. In 1908 a dinner was given in his honour in the Paris studio of Picasso, an event which marked the beginning of the artist's recognition as a painter of genius rather than simply a decorative painter in the 'primitive' style.

VINCENT VAN GOGH (1853–90)
Sunflowers
92.1 × 73 cm
Signed: *Vincent*

This is one of several paintings of sunflowers which Van Gogh painted towards the end of his life when he was living at Arles in Provence. At this time in his life he suffered from repeated bouts of insanity and finally shot himself in July 1890.

The startlingly brilliant colour in these several paintings of sunflowers may readily be seen as an expression of the tormented state of the artist's mind at this time.

PIERRE-AUGUSTE RENOIR (1841–1919)
Les Parapluies
180.3 × 114.9 cm

It is Paris in the 1880s and a crowd bustles with umbrellas in the rain. A snub-nosed girl in the centre lowers her umbrella and looks to see if the shower is over; a fashionable mother hurries her dallying children through the rain; and a *midinette* (a working girl who finishes work at mid-day) makes her way with a closed box on her arm.

The picture was painted in two stages (probably in 1881/2 and 1885/6) and the two parts are clearly recognizable by the difference in technique. The earlier part, the mother and the two little girls, is in an impressionistic style, and the remainder of the painting is more 'classical'. It was part of the Impressionists'

doctrine that the artist should paint what he sees without embellishment. Renoir therefore paints this scene in the rain without any formal composition as such; and by filling the figures out across the canvas he makes the spectator feel part of the scene portrayed. In that way the artist emphasizes the actuality of his subject: *La Vie Parisienne*.

Like other artists working in late nineteenth-century Paris, Renoir was influenced by the contemporary mania for things Japanese. The disregard for mathematical perspective apparent in Japanese prints led nineteenth-century painters to experiment with unusual viewpoints. Artists like Degas and Renoir became fascinated by the Japanese use of line and surface pattern. For Renoir Japanese ladies with parasols were easily translated into a contemporary Parisian crowd walking in the rain.

A Japanese print of the eighteenth century

A contemporary poster advertising
Miss La La's performance at the Cirque
Fernando, Paris

EDGAR DEGAS (1834–1917)
La La at the Cirque Fernando, Paris
116.8 × 77.5 cm
Signed: *degas*

'During the past week an additional attraction has been added in the person of a dusky lady known as La La, whose feats of strength fairly eclipse anything and everything of the kind that has gone before. She does all that her muscular rivals have done and a great deal more. She has we believe already astonished all Paris, and we have little doubt that her fame in London will rapidly spread.' Thus read the review of La La's performance at the Westminster Aquarium in March 1879. It was in January in that same year that Degas had made sketches of her when she performed at the Cirque Fernando on the Boulevard Roche-

chouart in Paris; and the National Gallery's picture was exhibited in Paris later that year.

It was from about the middle of the 1870s that Degas favoured the use of unusual viewpoints in his paintings. Taking his themes from contemporary Parisian life, ballet girls, cabaret artistes and women at their toilet, he was also interested in the new technique of photography. Looking at this image of La La, suspended momentarily from the ceiling, it is not difficult to see it as a painted snapshot. The composition is unusual: we are left to imagine the gasping crowd who witness her performance, while the rope from which she is suspended, unattached within the framework of the picture, is but a taut line from top to bottom.

Degas was a marvellous draughtsman, and perhaps more than any of his contemporaries he experimented with colour, technique and

the effects of light and form. In his later life, when he suffered increasing blindness, he turned to painting with pastel and modelling sculptures in wax (many of which were subsequently cast in bronze).

PAUL CÉZANNE (1839–1906)
Bathers
127.2 × 196.1 cm

From 1886, when his father died, Cézanne was wealthy enough to live in relative seclusion near Aix-en-Provence where he had been born. Throughout his life he had been attracted by the Renaissance theme of nude figures in a landscape, and although ill equipped as a draughtsman to paint the nude, he painted several pictures of bathers, generally on a small

scale. Between 1895 and his death in 1906, however, he painted three very large versions of the subject, the earliest of which is probably the present picture. Unable to find a model in Provence, or rather unwilling to scandalize the neighbourhood by painting nudes from the life, Cézanne used for the pictures studies from the nude which he had made many years previously. In spite of this the draughtsmanship in each of the three pictures remains very distorted.

Unlike the Impressionists, who sought to render the surface of objects, Cézanne's approach was more analytical and he attempted to model his forms through colour alone. Two of his large paintings of bathers, including this one, were exhibited in Paris at the Salon d'Automne in 1907 and were decisive influences on the development of Cubist painting as practised by Braque and Picasso.

PAUL CÉZANNE (1839–1906)
The Painter's Father
167.6 × 114.3 cm

In 1859, when Cézanne was twenty, his father
bought the property known as the Jas-de-
Bouffon outside Aix-en-Provence. At this time
the painter, on the insistence of his father, was
studying law at the University of Aix in prep-
aration for a career in the family banking
business. Cézanne's own wish, much opposed
by his father, was to go to Paris and study art,
and this he finally did, dropping his legal
studies, in April 1861.

Among the painter's very earliest works are
four pictures, now in the Petit Palais, Paris,
which he painted on the walls of the salon in
the Jas-de-Bouffon. As he signed one of these
'Ingres' and dated it 1811, they were probably
satirical in intention and likely to have been
painted very soon after his father's purchase of
the house. This portrait of his father reading a
newspaper, which comes from the same room,
was in all likelihood painted soon afterwards,
and is therefore also very early work.

The picture is painted in oil on top of the
ordinary housepaint which covered the plaster
of the walls. The paint, together with a very
thin layer of plaster, was removed about 1907
and mounted on canvas.

GUSTAV KLIMT (1862–1918)
Portrait of Hermine Gallia (illustrated in its frame)
170.5 × 96.5 cm
Signed: *Gustav Klimt 1904*

Hermine Gallia was the wife of Moritz Gallia, a Viennese *avant-garde* art patron. The portrait was painted in 1904. Klimt, principally a painter of decorative schemes, was the most important Jugendstil, or Art Nouveau, painter in Austria and one of the founders of the Vienna Secession movement, a group of artists who consciously rejected the academic style prevalent in the late nineteenth century. A feature of the movement was that it was concerned with all aspects of design, including that of everyday objects. In this case Klimt also designed the dress the sitter is wearing.

GEORGES-PIERRE SEURAT (1859–91)
Bathers, Asnières
201 × 300 cm
Signed: *Seurat*

When submitted to the Salon in 1884 the picture was refused and it remained in the artist's possession until his death at the age of thirty-two in 1891. The clump of trees on the right of the painting is the island called La Grande Jatte at Asnières, which is on the Seine, north of Paris.

Seurat studied at the Ecole des Beaux-Arts in Paris from 1877 and early became interested in scientific theories of colour. He evolved a theory, called Divisionism or Pointillism, whereby primary colours, applied in small dots, were intended to mingle in the eye of the spectator to create secondary colours.

Une Baignade, Asnières, which is the French title of this picture, was painted in 1883/4 before Seurat had evolved his theories fully, and in the picture different methods of painting are combined. The outlines of the figures are precisely, almost academically, drawn and indeed Seurat made elaborate crayon studies for all of the principal figures in the picture. The water is Impressionistic in style and parts of the picture, for example the orange hat of the boy in the water, were later reworked by the artist in a Divisionist technique.

It was in another picture, *Sunday Afternoon on the Grande Jatte* (now in Chicago), that Seurat put his theories of colour fully into practice. That picture, exhibited at the last Impressionist Exhibition in 1886, led to Seurat's style (and that of his followers) being called Neo-Impressionism.

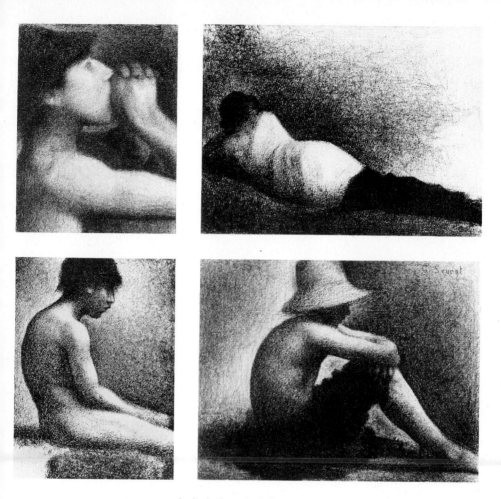

Studies by Seurat for *Bathers*, *Asnières*
(Yale University Art Gallery and a Private Collection)

Complete Catalogue of the Paintings in the National Gallery

A Number in **bold type** indicates the page on which a painting is illustrated
Reproductions in the catalogue illustrate works listed in the adjacent text

Antonello da Messina: S. Jerome
in his Study

Austrian School, 15th century:
The Trinity with Christ Crucified

Follower of Fra Angelico: The Rape of Helen by Paris

AACK, Johannes van der
(c. 1636–80)
An Old Woman seated Sewing

ALLORI, Alessandro (1535–1607)
ascribed to
A Knight of S. Stefano

ALTDORFER, Albrecht
(c. 1480–1538)
Landscape with a Footbridge

AMSTEL, Jan van (active 1527–
c. 1543) – after
Itinerant Entertainers in a Brothel

ANDREA di Aloigi, called
L'Ingegno (c.1484–c. 1516)
ascribed to
The Virgin and Child

ANDREA di Bonaiuto da Firenze
(active c. 1343–c. 1377)
ascribed to
The Virgin and Child with Ten Saints

ANDRIEU, Pierre (1821–92)
ascribed to
Still Life with Fruit and Flowers

ANGELICO, Fra (active 1417–55)
*Christ Glorified in the Court of
Heaven*

ANGELICO, Fra – ascribed to
Roundel: *A Martyr Bishop or Abbot*

ANGELICO, Fra – follower of
*The Adoration of the Kings
The Rape of Helen by Paris
Altarpiece: The Annunciation
The Vision of the Dominican Habit
The Virgin and Child with Angels*

ANTONELLO da Messina (active
1456–79)
*Salvator Mundi
Portrait of a Man*   4
*Christ Crucified
S. Jerome in his Study*

ANTONELLO da Messina – follower
of
The Virgin and Child

ARENTSZ, Arent (c. 1586 – c. 1635
Fishermen near Muiden Castle

AUGSBURG (?) School, 16th century
Portrait of a Man

AUSTRIAN School, 15th century
The Trinity with Christ Crucified

AVERCAMP, Hendrick (1585–1634)
*A Winter Scene with Skaters near a
Castle
A Scene on the Ice near a Town*

BACCHIACCA (1495–1557)
*The History of Joseph. I
The History of Joseph. II*

BACCHIACCA – ascribed to
Marcus Curtius

BADALOCCHIO, Sisto (1585–c. 162
Christ Carried to the Tomb

·BAKHUIZEN, Ludolf (1631–1708)
*Dutch Men-of-War and small Vessel
off Enkhuizen
The 'Eendracht' and a Fleet of Dutch
Men-of-War
A Beach Scene with Fishermen
An English Vessel and a Man-of-W
in rough Sea
A View across the River near
Dordrecht (?)*

Barbari: A Sparrowhawk

Batoni: Time orders Old Age to Destroy Beauty

Gentile Bellini: A Man with a Pair of Dividers

Giovanni Bellini: The Virgin and Child

Giovanni Bellini: S. Dominic

Berchem: Peasants with Cattle by a ruined Aqueduct

A Man in Profile

BOLTRAFFIO, Giovanni Antonio
  follower of
The Virgin and Child
Narcissus

BONFIGLI, Benedetto (active
  1445–96)
The Adoration of the Kings, Christ on
  the Cross

BONHEUR, Rosa (1822–99) and
  Micas, Nathalie
The Horse Fair

BONIFAZIO di Pitati (1487–1553)
Madonna and Child with S. James the
  Greater. Jerome, Infant Baptist and
  Catherine of Alexandria

BONIFAZIO di Pitati – studio of
A Huntsman

BONIFAZIO di Pitati – style of
The Labours of the Months: January
  to June; July to December
Madonna and Child with SS. John the
  Baptist, Elizabeth and Catherine of
  Alexandria

BONIFAZIO di Pitati – after
Dives and Lazarus

BONO da Ferrara (active 1442?–61?)
S. Jerome in a Landscape

BONSIGNORI, Francesco
  (1455?–1519?)
Portrait of an elderly Man
The Virgin and Child with four Saints

BONVIN, François (1817–87)
The Pasturage
Still Life

BORCH, Gerard ter (1617–81)
A Woman making Music with two
  Men
The Swearing of the Oath of
  Ratification of the Treaty of
  Münster
Portrait of a young Man
Portrait of Hermanna van der Cruis
An Officer dictating a Letter

BORDON, Paris (1500–71)
Daphnis and Chloe
Portrait of a young Lady
Christ as Light of the World
Christ baptising S. John Martyr,
  Duke of Alexandria

Giovanni Bellini: The Madonna of the Meadow

Berckheyde: The Market Place at Haarlem

ter Borch: The Swearing of the Oath of Ratification of the Treaty of Münster

173

Bosch: Christ Mocked (The Crowning with Thorns)

Botticelli: Mystic Nativity

Botticelli: Tondo: The Adoration of the Kings

BRESCIAN School, 16th century
The Death of S. Peter Martyr
'The Garden of Love'
Adoration of the Shepherds
Madonna and Child

BRESCIANINO, Andrea del (living
1506–c. 1525) and Raffaello del
(living 1506–45)
*Madonna and Child with the Infant
Baptist(?) and SS. Paul and
Catherine of Siena*

BRONZINO, Agnolo (1503–72)
An Allegory   72
*Portrait of Piero de' Medici ('The
Gouty')*
*Madonna and Child with the Baptist
and S. Anne or S. Elizabeth*

BRONZINO – studio of
*Portrait of Cosimo I de' Medici,
Grand Duke of Tuscany*

BRONZINO – follower of
Portrait of a Lady

BROUWER, Adriaen (1606?–38)
Four Peasants in a Cellar

BROWN, John Lewis (1829–90)
The performing Dog

BRUEGEL the Elder, Pieter (active
1551–69)
The Adoration of the Kings   59

BRUEGEL, Jan I (1568–1625)
The Adoration of the Kings

BRUGGHEN, Hendrick ter
(1588?–1629)
*Jacob reproaching Laban for giving him
Leah in Place of Rachel*
A Man playing a Lute   115

BRUSSEL, Paulus Theodorus van
(1754–95)
Flowers in a Vase
Flowers in a Vase
Fruit and Flowers

BRUYN the Elder, Bartholomeus
(1492/5–1555)
A Man of the Strauss(?) Family
*The Virgin, S. John, S. Mary
Magdalene and a Holy Woman*

BUONCONSIGLIO, Giovanni (active
1495–1535/7)
S. John the Baptist

Boucher: Landscape with a Watermill

Boudin: Beach Scene, Trouville

BUSATI, Andrea (active 1503–28)
The Entombment

BUTINONE, Bernardino (active
1485–1507) – ascribed to
The Adoration of the Shepherds

BUYTEWEGH the Younger, Willem
(1625–70)
A Dune Landscape

BYZANTINE School, 17th century
Noli Me Tangere

BYZANTINE School, c. 1800(?)
Entombment of the Virgin

CALAME, Alexandre (1810–64)
The Lake of Thun

CALRAET, Abraham van
(1642–1722)
A Horse with a Saddle nearby
The Interior of a Stable
Scene on the Ice outside Dordrecht

Bouts: The Entombment

Campin: A Man

Campin: A Woman

Canaletto: Eton College

Cappelle: A Shipping Scene with a Dutch Yacht firing a Salute

CAMPIN, Robert (1378/9–1444)
The Virgin and Child before a
Firescreen
Portrait of a Man

CAMPIN, Robert – ascribed to
A Man
A Woman

CAMPIN, Robert – after (?)
The Virgin and Child with two Angels

CAMPIN, Robert – imitator of
(early 16th century ?)
The Death of the Virgin

CANALETTO, Giovanni Antonio
Canal, called (1697–1768)
Venice: Campo S. Vidal and S.
Maria della Carita **133**
Venice: Upper Reaches of the Grand
Canal with S. Simeone Piccolo
Venice: The Feastday of S. Roch
Venice: A Regatta on the Grand
Canal
Eton College
London: Interior of the Rotunda at
Ranelagh
Venice: Piazza S. Marco
Venice: Piazza S. Marco and the
Colonnade of the Procuratie Nuove
Venice: The Basin of S. Marco on
Ascension Day **132**
Venice: A Regatta on the Grand
Canal

CANALETTO, Giovanni Antonio
studio of
Venice: The Piazzetta from the Molo
Venice: The Doge's Palace and the
Riva Degli Schiavoni
Venice: Palazzo Grimani
Venice: Entrance to the Cannaregio
Venice: S. Pietro in Castello

CANALETTO, Giovanni Antonio
follower of
Venice: S. Simeone Piccolo
Venice: Upper Reaches of the Grand
Canal facing S. Croce
Venice: Upper Reaches of the Grand
Canal facing S. Croce

CAPPELLE, Jan Van de
(c. 1623/5–79)
A Small Vessel in light Airs
Vessels in light Airs
A Shipping Scene with a Dutch Yacht
firing a Salute

Canaletto: Venice: Piazza S. Marco and the Colonnade of the Procuratie Nuove

Annibale Carracci: Christ appearing to S. Peter on the Appian Way

Cézanne: An Old Woman with a Rosary

Claude: Landscape: Hagar and
the Angel

Petrus Christus: Portrait
of a young Man

Constable: The Cornfield

Cuyp: A Milkmaid and Cattle near Dordrecht

Degas: Beach Scene

David: Christ nailed to the Cross

Crivelli: The Annunciation, with
S. Emidius

Domenichino: S. George killing
the Dragon

Domenichino: Apollo pursuing Daphne

Drouais: Le Comte de Vaudreuil

Dosso Dossi: The Adoration of the
Kings

Van Dyck: The Emperor Theodosius
forbidden entry to Milan Cathedral

Van Dyck: Lady Elizabeth Thimbelby
and Dorothy, Viscountess Andover

Florentine School, 15th century: The Combat of Love and Chastity

Francia: The Virgin and Child with S. Anne and other Saints

Gainsborough: The Painter's Daughters chasing a Butterfly

Wing of a Diptych: *The Dead Christ and the Virgin*
The Baptism of Chist

FLORENTINE School, 15th century
The Combat of Love and Chastity
Tondo: *The Virgin and Child, S. John and an Angel*
Tondo: *The Holy Family with Angels*
The Virgin and Child with two Angels
Roundel: *God the Father*
Cassone, with the Story of the *Schoolmaster of Falerii*
SS. Catherine and Bartholomew
The Virgin and Child

FLORENTINE(?) School, 15th century
Portrait of a young Man

FLORENTINE School, 16th century
Portrait of a Lady
A Knight of S. John

(?)FLORENTINE School, 16th century
Portrait of a Lady
Portrait of a Boy
A Bearded Man
Portrait of Savonarola

FONTAINEBLEAU School, 16th century
Cleopatra

FOPPA, Vincenzo (active 1456–1515/16)
Altarpiece: *The Adoration of the Kings*

FORAIN, Jean-Louis (1852–1931)
Legal Assistance

FORTUNY, Mariano (1838–74)
The Bull-Fighter's Salute

FRAGONARD, Jean-Honoré (1732–1806) – ascribed to
Interior Scene

FRANCESCO di Antonio (c. 1394–1433 or later)
The Virgin and Child with six Angels and two Cherubim

FRANCESCO di Giorgio (1439–1510/12)
S. Dorothy and the Infant Christ

FRANCHOIJS, Peeter (1606–54) ascribed to
Portrait of Lucas Fayd' Herbe (?)

FRANCIA, Francesco (c. 1450–1517/18)
Altarpiece: *The Virgin and Child with S. Anne and other Saints:*
Lunette to above: *Pietà*
The Virgin and Child with two Saints
Bartolomeo Bianchini

FRANCIA, Francesco – ascribed to
Mourning over the dead Christ

FRANCIA, Francesco – after
The Virgin and Child with an Angel

FRANCIABIGIO (c. 1482/3–1525)
Portrait of a Knight of Rhodes

FRENCH(?) School, c. 1395 or later
Richard II presented to the Virgin and Child by his Patron Saints ('The Wilton Diptych')   2

FRENCH School (?), 15th century (?)
The Virgin

FRENCH School, 16th century
Paul, Sire D'Andouins (?)
Portrait of a Lady

FRENCH School (?), 16th century
Portrait of a Boy
Portrait of a Man

FRENCH School (?), 16th century (?)
Portrait of a Man
Portrait of a young Lady

FRENCH School (?), 17th century
The Visitation

FRENCH School, 18th century
Madame de Gléon (?)

FRENCH School, early 19th century
Portrait of a Boy

FRENCH School (?), early 19th century
An 'Académie'

FRENCH School (?), 19th century
A Black Woman

FROMENTIN, Eugène (1820–76)
The Banks of the Nile

FUNGAI, Bernardino (1460–c.1516)
Tondo: *The Virgin and Child with Cherubim*

FYT, Joannes (1611–61)
Dead Birds in a Landscape

FYT, Joannes – ascribed to
A Still Life with a Parrot

GADDI, Agnolo (active 1369–96)
ascribed to
Part(?) of an altarpiece: *The
Coronation of the Virgin*

GAINSBOROUGH, Thomas
(1727–88)
The Watering Place
Mrs Siddons
Dr Ralph Schomberg
*Gainsborough's Forest ('Cornard
Wood')*
*The Painter's Daughters chasing a
Butterfly*
The Painter's Daughters with a Cat
Pomeranian Bitch (?) and Puppy
John Plampin
The Morning Walk   **143**
Mr and Mrs Andrews   **145**

GARGIULO, Domenico (?)
(1612?–c.1675)
The Finding of Moses

GAROFALO (1481?–1559)
*S. Augustine with the Holy Family
and S. Catherine of Alexandria*
*The Holy Family with SS. John the
Baptist, Elizabeth, Zacharias and
Francis (?)*
The Agony in the Garden
*Madonna and Child with SS. William
of Aquitaine, Clare, Anthony of
Padua and Francis*
An Allegory of Love
S. Catherine of Alexandria
A Pagan Sacrifice

GAUDENZIO, Ferrari (active
1508–46)
Christ rising from the Tomb
The Annunciation
S. Andrew (?)

GAUGUIN, Paul (1848–1903)
Flower Piece

GEERTGEN tot Sint Jans (late 15th
century) – ascribed to
The Nativity, at Night

GÉRICAULT, Jean-Louis-André-
Théodore (1791–1824)
A Horse frightened by Lightning

GÉRICAULT, Jean-Louis-André-
Théodore – ascribed to
An 'Académie'

Gainsborough: The Watering Place

Gainsborough: John Plampin

Géricault: A Horse frightened by Lightning

Style of Domenico Ghirlandaio:
Costanza Caetani

GERMAN School, 16th century
Portrait of a Woman

GERMAN (?) School, 17th century
*S. Christopher carrying the Infant
Christ*

GERMAN School – ascribed to
*Virgin and Child with an Angel in a
Landscape*

GEROLAMO dai Libri
(*c.* 1474–1555?)
The Virgin and Child with S. Anne

GEROLAMO da Santacroce (active
1516–56?) – ascribed to
A Youthful Saint reading
A Saint with a Fortress and Banner

GEROLAMO da Vicenza (active
1488)
*The Death and Assumption of the
Virgin*

GÉRÔME, Jean-Léon (1824–1904)
A Student of the École Polytechnique

GHEYN III, Jacob de
(*c.* 1596–1641) – after
S. Paul reading

GHIRLANDAIO, Domenico
(*c.* 1448–94)
*A Legend of SS. Justus and Clement
of Volterra*

GHIRLANDAIO, Domenico
studio of
Portrait of a Girl
The Virgin and Child

Giorgione: Sunset Landscape with S. Roch(?), S. George and
S. Anthony Abbot

GHIRLANDAIO, Domenico
follower of
Portrait of a young Man in Red
The Virgin and Child with S. John

GHIRLANDAIO, Domenico
style of
Costanza Caetani

GHIRLANDAIO, Ridolfo
(1483–1561)
The Procession to Calvary
Portrait of a Man

GIAMBONO, Michele (active
1420–62)
Saint with a Book

GIAMPIETRINO (active first half
16th century)
Christ carrying his Cross
Salome

GIANNICOLA di Paolo (active
1484–1544) – ascribed to
The Annunciation

GIAQUINTO, Corrado (1703–66)
Apotheosis of the Spanish Monarchy (?)

GIBSON, John (1790–1866)
William Bewick (marble bust)

GIOLFINO, Niccolò
(*c.* 1476/7–1555) – ascribed to
*Portraits of the Giusti Family of
Verona (?)*

GIORDANO, Luca (1634–1705)
A Homage to Velázquez
*S. Anthony of Padua miraculously
restores the Foot of a self-mutilated
Man*
The Martyrdom of S. Januarius

GIORDANO, Luca – style of
The Toilet of Bathsheba

GIORGIONE (active 1506–10)
The Adoration of the Magi
*Sunset Landscape with S. Roch (?),
S. George and S. Anthony Abbot*

GIORGIONE – imitator of
A Man in Armour
Homage to a Poet
*Nymphs and Children in a Landscape
with Shepherds*

GIOTTO (1266?–1337) – ascribed to
Pentecost   **27**

Giordano: A Homage to Velázquez

Gossaert: The Adoration of the Kings

Goya: Don Andres del Peral

Guardi: An Architectural Caprice

Helst: Portrait of a Lady

Honthorst: Christ before
the High Priest

GRECO, EL – ascribed to
S. Jerome as Cardinal

GRECO, EL – studio of
*The Agony in the Garden of
Gethsemane*

GRECO, EL – after
S. Peter (?)

GRECO-ROMAN
A Young Woman
A Man with a Wreath
A Young Woman with a Wreath

GREUZE, Jean-Baptiste
(1725–1805)
A Girl
A Child with an Apple
A Girl with a Lamb

GREUZE, Jean-Baptiste
follower of
A Girl

GUARDI, Francesco (1712–93)
Venice: Piazza S. Marco
A Gondola on the Lagoon near Mestre
*Venice: The Punta della Dogana with
S. Maria della Salute*   **134**
*Venice: The Doge's Palace and the
Molo*
*An Architectural Caprice with a
Palladian-Style Building*
A Caprice with a ruined Arch
An Architectural Caprice
A View near Venice (?)
Caprice View, with Ruins
A Caprice with Ruins on the Seashore
An Architectural Caprice
*View on the Venetian Lagoon with the
Tower of Malghera*
Venice: Piazza S. Marco
Venice: The Arsenal
*Venice: The Grand Canal with
Palazzo Pesaro*
Venice: The Punta della Dogana
Venice: The Giudecca with the Zitelle

GUARDI, Francesco – imitator of
Venice: Entrance to the Cannaregio
A Ruin Caprice
A Ruin Caprice

GUERCINO (1591–1666)
Angels weeping over the dead Christ
The Incredulity of S. Thomas

GUERCINO – after
A Bearded Man holding a Lamp

HACCOU, Johannes Cornelis
(1798–1839)
A Road by a Cottage

HACKAERT, Johannes (1628/9–
c. 1685) and Nicolaes Berchem
A Stag Hunt

HAENSBERGEN, Johan van
(1642–1705) – ascribed to
Women bathing in a Landscape

HALS, Dirck (1591–1656)
A Party at a Table

HALS, Frans (c. 1580?–1666)
Portrait of a middle-aged Woman
Portrait of a Man in his Thirties
A Family Group in a Landscape **123**
Portrait of a Man
Portrait of a Woman
*Portrait of Jean de la Chambre at the
age of 33*
Portrait of a Woman

HARPIGNIES, Henri-Joseph
(1819–1916)
The Painter's Garden at Saint-Privé
A River Scene
Olive Trees at Menton
River and Hills
Autumn Evening

HEDA, Gerrit (active 1642–c. 1702)
Still Life
Still Life with a Lobster

HEEM, David Davidsz de (?)
(active 1668)
Still Life

HEIMBACH, Wolfgang
(active 1636–78)
Portrait of a young Man

HELST, Bartholomeus van der
(1613?–70)
Portrait of a Girl
Portrait of a Lady

HELST, Bartholomeus van der
ascribed to
Portrait of a Man

HEMESSEN, Katharina de (1527/8–
c. 1566?)
Portrait of a Man
Portrait of a Lady

HEMESSEN, Katharina de
ascribed to
A Lady with a Rosary

Guercino: The Incredulity of S. Thomas

Ingres: Angelica saved by Ruggiero

Jacometto: Portrait of a Boy

Jardin: Self-Portrait (?)

Joos: Music

ISRAËLS, Jozef (1824–1911)
An Old Man Writing
Fishermen carrying a drowned Man

ITALIAN School (?), 13th century
The Virgin and Child with two Angels

ITALIAN School, 16th century
The Attack on Cartagena
The Continence of Scipio
The Rape of the Sabines
The Reconciliation of Romans and Sabines
Portrait of a young Man
Portrait of a young Man
A Man and his Wife
A Jesse-Tree
The Holy Family
Portrait of a Lady with a Dog

ITALIAN School, 17th century
Bust Portrait of a bearded Man
Bust of a Man

ITALIAN School, 17th (?) century
An Old Man holding a Pilgrim-Bottle

ITALIAN School, 18th century
S. Catherine of Alexandria (?)

ITALIAN School (?), 17th (?) century
A Dead Soldier

ITALIAN (?) School, 17th (?) century
The Dying Alexander (porphyry)

ITALIAN School, 19th century ascribed to
Portrait of a Woman

ITALIAN School (various periods)
Portrait of a young Man
Bust of Andrea Mantegna in Relief
Portrait of an old Man
Portrait Group

JACKSON, John (1778–1831)
The Rev. William Holwell Carr
William Seguier

JACOMETTO Veneziano (active c. 1472–c. 1498)
Portrait of a Boy
Portrait of a Man

JANSSENS, Hieronymus (1624–93) follower of
'La Main Chaude'

JARDIN, Karel du (1621/2?–78)

A Landscape with Farm Animals
Peasants at a Ford
Farm Animals in an Italian Landscape
Sheep and Goats
Self-Portrait (?)
The Conversion of S. Paul

JOHNSON, Cornelius (1593–1661)
Portrait of a Lady

JONGKIND, Johan Barthold (1818–91)
Skating in Holland
River Scene

Joos van Wassenhove (active 1460–c. 1480/85)
Rhetoric (?)
Music

JORDAENS, Jacob (1593–1678)
The Holy Family and S. John the Baptist
The Virgin and Child with S.S. Zacharias, Elizabeth and John the Baptist
Govaert van Surpele (?) and his wife   102

JUAN de Flandes (active 1496–c. 1519) – studio of
Christ appearing to the Virgin with the Redeemed of the Old Testament

JUEL, Jens (1745–1802)
Joseph Greenway

KESSEL, Johan van (?) (1641/2–80)
A Torrent in a mountainous Landscape

KEYSER, Thomas de (1596/7–1667)
Constantijn Huygens and his (?) Clerk   124

KEYSER, Thomas de – ascribed to
Portrait of a Man and a Woman

KLIMT, Gustav (1862–1918)
Portrait of Hermine Gallia   167

KONINCK, Philips (1619–88)
A Landscape with a Hawking Party
An Extensive Landscape with Houses in a Wood
An Extensive Landscape with a Road by a Ruin   118
An Extensive Landscape with a Town in the middle Distance

LA FARGUE, Paulus Constantijn (1729–82)
The Grote Markt at the Hague

Lastman: Juno discovering Jupiter with Io

La Tour: Henry Dawkins

Filippino Lippi: The Virgin and Child with
SS. Jerome and Dominic

Fra Filippo Lippi: The Annunciation

Liss: Judith in the Tent
of Holofernes

LEYDEN School, latter half of the
17th century
A Young Astronomer

LEYSTER, Judith (1609–60)
A Boy and a Girl

LIBERALE da Verona (*c.* 1445–
c. 1526)
The Virgin and Child with two Angels
Dido's Suicide

LICINIO, Bernardino (*c.* 1491–
c. 1549)
Portrait of Stefano Nani
Madonna and Child with S. Joseph
and a female Martyr

LIEVENSZ, Jan (1607–74)
A Landscape with Tobias and the
Angel
Portrait of Anna Maria Schurman
Self-Portrait

LINGELBACH, Johannes (1622–74)
Peasants loading a Hay Cart

LINNELL, John (1792–1882)
Samuel Rogers

LIOTARD, Jean-Étienne (1702–89)
A Grand Vizir (?)

LIPPI, Filippino (1457?–1504)
Altarpiece: *The Virgin and Child*
with SS. Jerome and Dominic
An Angel adoring (fragment)
The Adoration of the Kings
The Virgin and Child with S. John
Moses brings forth Water out of the
Rock
The Worship of the Egyptian Bull-
God, Apis

LIPPI, Fra Filippo (*c.* 1406?–69)
S. Bernard's Vision of the Virgin
The Annunciation
Seven Saints

LIPPI, Fra Filippo – ascribed to
The Virgin and Child

LIPPO di Dalmasio (*c.* 1352?–
*c.*1410)
'The Madonna of Humility'

LISS, Johann (*c.* 1595–1629/30)
Judith in the Tent of Holofernes

LOCHNER, Stephan (active
1442–51)
SS. Matthew, Catherine of
Alexandria and John the Evangelist

LONGHI, Alessandro (1733–1813)
Caterina Penza

LONGHI, Pietro (1702?–85)
An Interior with three Woman and a
seated Man
Exhibition of a Rhinoceros at
Venice **13**
A Fortune-Teller at Venice
A Lady receiving a Cavalier
A Nobleman kissing a Lady's Hand

LOOTEN, Jan (*c.* 1618–*c.*1680?)
A River Landscape

LORENZETTI, Ambrogio (active
1319–47)
Fresco: *A Group of Poor Clares*
(fragment)

Lochner: SS. Matthew, Catherine of
Alexandria and John the Evangelist

Manet: The Waitress

Manet: Eva Gonzales

Mantegna: Samson and Delilah

Masolino: SS. John the Baptist
and Jerome

MASTER OF THE DEATH OF THE
VIRGIN (active 1507–37)
The Holy Family

MASTER OF THE DEATH OF THE
VIRGIN – after
The Adoration of the Kings

MASTER OF THE DEATH OF THE
VIRGIN – follower of
The Crucifixion
The Annunciation

MASTER OF DELFT (early 16th
century)
Scenes from the Passion

MASTER OF THE FEMALE HALF-
LENGTHS – studio of
S. John on Patmos
The Rest on the Flight to Egypt

MASTER OF THE FEMALE HALF-
LENGTHS – ascribed to the
studio of
A Female Head

MASTER OF THE FEMALE HALF-
LENGTHS – style of
*S. Christopher carrying the Infant
Christ*

MASTER OF LIESBORN (latter half
15th century)
*From The Liesborn Altarpiece: The
Annunciation; The Presentation in
the Temple; The Adoration of the
Kings; Head of Christ Crucified;
SS. John the Evangelist, Scholastic
and Benedict; SS. Cosmas and
Damian and the Virgin*

MASTER OF LIESBORN – circle of
S. Ambrose, Exuperius and Jerome
S. Gregory, Maurice and Augustine
The Crucifixion with Saints
The Virgin and Child with a Donor
S. Dorothy
S. Margaret

MASTER OF THE LIFE OF THE
VIRGIN (latter half 15th century)
The Presentation in the Temple

MASTER OF THE LIFE OF THE
VIRGIN – studio of
*S. Jerome, Bernard (?) Giles and
Benedict (?)*
*S. Augustine, Ludger (?), Hubert
and Gereon (?)*
The Conversion of S. Hubert   **53**
The Mass of S. Hubert

MASTER OF THE MAGDALEN
LEGEND (late 15th–early 16th
century) – studio of
The Magdalen

MASTER OF THE MANSI MAGDALEN
(early 16th century)
Judith and the infant Hercules

MASTER OF MOULINS (active
c. 1483–*c.* 1500) – studio of
*Charlemagne, and the Meeting of
SS. Joachim and Anne at the
Golden Gate*

MASTER OF THE OSSERVANZA
(active *c.* 1436)
Triptych: *The Birth of the Virgin*

MASTER OF THE PALA SFORZESCA
(active *c.* 1495) – ascribed to
S. Paul
*The Virgin and Child with Saints and
Donors*

MASTER OF THE PRODIGAL SON
(active 1535?–*c.* 1560)
ascribed to the studio of
Pietà

MASTER OF RIGLOS (mid-15th
century)
The Crucifixion

MASTER OF THE S. BARTHOLOMEW
ALTARPIECE (active late
15th/early 16th century)
SS. Peter and Dorothy

MASTER OF SAINT GILES (active
c. 1500)
S. Giles and the Hind
The Mass of S. Giles

MASTER OF THE S. URSULA
LEGEND (active late 15th/early
16th century) – circle of
*S. Lawrence showing the Prefect the
Treasures of the Church*

MASTER OF S. VERONICA (active
early 15th century) – circle of
S. Veronica with the Sudarium

MASTER OF SAN FRANCESCO (end
13th century) – ascribed to
Crucifix

MASTER OF THE STORY OF
GRISELDA (16th century)
The Story of Patient Griselda

Massys: The Virgin and Child
enthroned, with four Angels

Master of Liesborn: The
Presentation in the Temple

Master of S. Veronica: S. Veronica
with the Sudarium

Matteo di Giovanni: S. Sebastian

Memlinc: A Young Man at Prayer

MIERIS, Willem van (1662–1747)
A Woman and a Fish-Pedlar

MIGNARD, Pierre (1612–95)
The Marquise de Seignelay and two of her Children

MIGNARD, Pierre – ascribed to
Portrait of a Man

MILANESE School, 15th century
The Virgin and Child
Bona of Savoy (?)

MILLET, Francisque (1642–79)
Mountain Landscape, with Lightning

MILLET, Jean-François (1814–75)
The Whisper

MILLET, Jean-François
ascribed to
Landscape with Buildings

MOCETTO, Gerolamo (c. 1458–1531)
The Massacre of the Innocents (two fragments (?))

MOLA, Pier Francesco (1612–66)
S. John the Baptist preaching in the Wilderness
The Rest on the Flight into Egypt

MOLA, Pier Francesco – style of
Leda and the Swan

MOLENAER, Jan (1609–68)
A Young Man and Woman making Music
Children making Music

MOMPER II, Joos de – follower of (1564–1635)
A Music Party before a Village

MONET, Claude-Oscar (1840–1926)
Lavacourt (?), Winter
The Beach at Trouville
The Water-Lily Pond
Flood Water
Water Lilies   160
Irises
River Scene
The Thames below Westminster   158

MONTAGNA, Bartolomeo (1459–1523)
The Virgin and Child
Three Saints

Mola: S. John the Baptist preaching in the Wilderness

Monet: The Beach at Trouville

Monet: The Water-Lily Pond

Moretto da Brescia: Portrait of a Man

Murillo: Self-Portrait

Murillo: A Peasant Boy leaning
on a Sill

MONTAGNA, Bartolomeo
ascribed to
The Virgin and Child
Fresco: *The Virgin and Child*

MONTICELLI, Adolphe (1824–86)
The Hayfield
Sunrise
Sunset
Torchlight Procession
Subject Composition
Fountain in a Park
Meeting Place of the Hunt
Still Life: Oysters and Fish
Still Life: Fruit
Wild Flowers
Subject Composition
Conversation Piece
Subject Composition

MOR Van Dashorst, Anthonis
(active 1544–76/7)
Portrait of a Man

MORALES, Luis de (active
1546–86?)
The Virgin and Child

MORANDO, Paolo (*c.* 1486–1522)
S. Roch
*The Virgin and Child, S. John the
Baptist and an Angel*

MOREAU, Gustave (1826–98)
S. George and the Dragon

MORETTO da Brescia (*c.* 1498–1554)
Portrait of a Man
Altarpiece: *Madonna and Child with
S. Bernardino and other Saints*
Portrait of a Gentleman
Altarpiece: *Madonna and Child with
SS. Hippolytus and Catherine of
Alexandria*
Madonna and Child with Saints
*Portrait of a Member of the Averoldi
Family (?)*
Christ Blessing S. John the Baptist

MORISOT, Berthe (1841–95)
Summer's Day

MORONE, Domenico (*c.* 1442–
c. 1517)
Scene at a Tournament
Scene at a Tournament

MORONE, Francesco (*c.* 1471–1529)
The Virgin and Child

MORONI, Giovan Battista (active
1546–78)
Portrait of a Man ('The Tailor')
Portrait of a Man holding a Letter
Portrait of a Gentleman
Portrait of a Lady
Canon Ludovico di Terzi
Portrait of a Gentleman
Portrait of a Gentleman
Chastity
Leonardo Salvagno (?)
Portrait of a Man
Count Lupi (?)

MORONI, Giovan Battista
ascribed to
An Angel
An Angel
S. Joseph
S. Jerome

MOSTAERT, Jan (*c.* 1475–1556)
*The Head of S. John the Baptist, with
mourning Angels and Putti*

MOSTAERT, Jan – style of
Christ crowned with Thorns

MOUCHERON, Frederick de
(1633–86)
Figures in an Italian Garden
A Landscape with classical Ruins

MURILLO, Bartolomé Esteban
(1617–82)
*The Two Trinities ('The Pedrose
Murillo')*
A Peasant Boy leaning on a Sill
The Infant S. John with the Lamb
*Christ healing the Paralytic at the Poc
of Bethesda* 10
Self-Portrait

MURILLO, Bartolomé Esteban
ascribed to
The Adoration of the Shepherds

MURILLO, Bartolomé Esteban
after
The Birth of the Virgin

MURILLO, Bartolomé Esteban –
follower of
*The Immaculate Conception of the
Virgin*
S. John Baptist in the Wilderness

MURILLO, Bartolomé Esteban –
style of
A Young Man drinking

NARDO di Cione (active *c.* 1343–
   c. 1365)
Altarpiece: *Three Saints*

NATTIER, Jean-Marc (1685–1766)
Manon Balletti
Bust of a Man in Armour

NAZARI, Narzario (1724–*c.* 1793)
Andrea Tron

NEAPOLITAN School, 17th century
Christ disputing with the Doctors

NEAPOLITAN School, 18th century
Portrait of a Lady

NEEFFS I, Peeter (active 1605–
   c. 1660)
View of a Chapel at Evening

NEEFFS I, Peeter, and PEETERS I,
   Bonaventura
An Evening Service in a Church

NEER, Aernout (Aert) van der
   (1630–77)
An Evening View near a Village
A Moonlit View
An Evening View along a River
A Frozen River near a Town
Golfers and Skaters near a Village
A Landscape with a River at Evening
A River Landscape with a Village
A Village by a River in Moonlight
*An Evening Landscape with a Horse
   and Cart*

NEER, Eglon Hendrik van der
   (1634?–1703)
Judith

NETHERLANDISH School, 15th
   century
*S. Ambrose with Ambrosius van
   Engelen (?)*
The Virgin and Child
A Girl writing
The Magdalen
A Man with a Pansy and a Skull
A Young Man praying
*The Virgin and Child with Saints and
   Angels in a Garden*
The Virgin and Child with S. Anne
A Man
Landscape: A River among Mountains
Mevr. van der Goes, née van Spangen
The Virgin and Child in a Landscape
*Edzard the Great, Count of East
   Friesland (1462–1528)*

Portrait of a bearded Man
A Young Man holding a Ring
*Philip the Fair and his Sister
   Margaret of Austria*
The Magdalen (?)
The Virgin and Child enthroned
The Magdalen weeping
The Virgin and Child with two Angels
The Birth of the Virgin (?)
Acts of Charity (?)
*A Little Girl with a Basket of
   Cherries*
*Portrait of a Man aged 42: a Member
   of Boulengé de la Hainière Family*

NETSCHER, Caspar (1635–84)
Two Boys blowing Bubbles
A Lady teaching a Child to Read
A Lady at a Spinning Wheel
Portrait of a Lady and a Girl
Portrait of a Lady

NETSCHER, Caspar – studio of
Portrait of a young Man

NETSCHER, Caspar – after
A Musical Party

NEUFCHÂTEL, Nicolas de (active
   1561–7)
Portrait of a young Lady

NEUFCHÂTEL, Nicolas de
   style of
A Man with a Skull

NICCOLO dell'Abate (*c.* 1509–71)
   ascribed to
The Story of Aristaeus   **89**

NICCOLÒ di Buonaccorso (active
   1372–88)
The Marriage of the Virgin

NICCOLÒ di Liberatore (active
   1456–1502)
Triptych: *Christ on the Cross, and
   other Scenes*

NICCOLÒ di Pietro Gerini (active
   1368–1415) – ascribed to
Triptych: *the Baptism of Christ, with
   SS. Peter and Paul*

NOMÉ, François de (1593–*c.* 1644?)
*Fantastic Ruins with Saint Augustine
   and the Child*

NORTH GERMAN School,
   16th–17th century
Christ carrying the Cross

Nattier: Manon Balletti

Netherlandish School: The
Magdalen weeping

Netscher: Two Boys blowing Bubbles

Parmigianino: Altarpiece: Madonna and Child with SS. John the Baptist and Jerome

Perugino: The Virgin and Child with S. John

NORTH ITALIAN School, 16th century
The Adoration of the Magi
S. Hugh
Portrait of a Musician
Portrait of a Man in a large black Hat
Portrait of a Lady in a plumed Hat

NORTH ITALIAN School, 17th century
The Adoration of the Shepherds
A Man holding an armless Statuette

NORTH ITALIAN School, 18th century – ascribed to
The Interior of a Theatre

NOUTS, Michiel (?) (active 1656)
A Family Group

OCHTERVELT, Jacob (1652–c. 1710)
A Woman by a Harpsichord
A Young Lady Trimming her Finger Nails
A Musical Party

OLIS, Jan (c. 1610?–76)
A Musical Party

OOST I, Jacques van (1601–71)
A Boy aged Eleven

OOST I, Jacques van – ascribed to
Two Boys before an Easel

ORCAGNA (Andrea di Cione) (active 1343–69) – style of
Altarpiece: *The Coronation of the Virgin, with Adoring Saints*
The Trinity
Seraphim, Cherubim and Angels Adoring
The Adoration of the Shepherds
The Adoration of the Kings
The Resurrection
The Maries at the Sepulchre
The Ascension
Pentecost
Small altarpiece: *The Crucifixion*
'*Noli Me Tangere*'

ORLEY, Bernaert van (c. 1488?–1541) – style of
The Virgin and Child in a Landscape

ORSI, Lelio (c. 1511–87) ascribed to
The Walk to Emmaus

ORTOLANO, L' (c. 1487–c. 1524)
Altarpiece: *SS. Sebastian, Roch and Demetrius*

Os, Georgius Jacobus Johannes van (1782–1861)
Fruit, Flowers and Game

Os, Jan van (1744–1808)
Fruit, Flowers and a Fish
Dutch Vessels in calm Water

OSTADE, Adriaen van (1610–85)
An Alchemist
An Interior of an Inn
Two Peasants
A Peasant holding a Jug

OSTADE, Adriaen van – after
A Cobbler

OSTADE, Isack van (1621–49)
The Outskirts of a Village
A Winter Scene
A Farmyard
Peasants and a Cart
The Interior of a Barn with two Peasants

OSTADE, Isack van – style of
An Inn by a frozen River

PACCHIAROTTO, Giacomo (1474–c. 1540) – ascribed to
Altarpiece: *the Nativity with Saints*

PACHER, Michael (active 1465?–98) circle of
The Virgin and Child enthroned with Angels and Saints

PADOVANINO (1588–1648) – after
Cornelia and her Sons

PALMA Giovane (1544–1628)
Mars and Venus

PALMA Vecchio (active 1510–28)
Portrait of a Poet, probably Ariosto
A Blond Woman

PALMA Vecchio – ascribed to
S. George and a female Saint

PALMEZZANO, Marco (c. 1458–1539)
The Dead Christ in the Tomb, with the Virgin Mary and Saints

PANINI, Giovanni Paolo (c. 1692–1765?)
Roman Ruins with Figures
Rome: The Interior of S. Peter's

PAOLO da San Leocadio (active 1472–1520)
The Virgin and Child with Saints

PAPE, Abraham de (*c.* 1621?–66)
Tobit and Anna (?)

PARMIGIANINO (1503–40)
Altarpiece: *Madonna and Child with
SS. John the Baptist and Jerome
The Mystic Marriage of
S. Catherine*   77

PATENIER, Joachim (active 1515–
c. 1524) – ascribed to
S. Jerome in a rocky Landscape   **61**

PATENIER, Joachim – studio of
*Landscape with the Rest on the Flight
into Egypt*

PATENIER, Joachim – style of
*The Virgin and Child with a
Cistercian Nun* (?)

Pellegrini: An Allegory of the Marriage of the Elector Palatine

PATER, Jean-Baptiste (1695–1736)
imitator of
'*La Danse*'

PELLEGRINI, Giovanni Antonio
(1675–1741)
*An Allegory of the Marriage of the
Elector Palatine
Rebecca at the Well*

PERRONNEAU, Jean-Baptiste
(1715?–83)
*A Girl with a Kitten
Madame Legrix* (?)
Portrait of Jacques Cazotte   **137**

PERUGINO, Pietro (living
1469–1523)
The Virgin and Child with S. John
Three panels of an altarpiece: *The
Virgin and Child with SS. Raphael
and Michael*
Altarpiece: *The Virgin and Child
with SS. Francis and Jerome*

PERUGINO, Pietro – after
The Baptism of Christ

PERUGINO, Pietro – follower of
*The Virgin and Child in a Mandorla
with Cherubim
The Virgin and Child, with SS.
Dominic and Catherine of Siena,
and two Donors*

PERUZZI, Baldassare (1481–1536)
The Adoration of the Magi

PESELLINO (*c.* 1422–57)
Altarpiece: *The Trinity with Saints*

Pesellino: The Trinity with Saints

Piero della Francesca: The Nativity

Pontormo: Joseph in Egypt

Preti: The Marriage at Cana

Pittoni: The Nativity with God the Father and the Holy Ghost

POLLAIUOLO, Antonio and Piero del (*c.* 1432–98; *c.* 1441–96) ascribed to
Altarpiece: *The Martyrdom of S. Sebastian*   **35**
Apollo and Daphne

PONTORMO (1494–1557)
Joseph in Egypt
A Discussion

PONTORMO – ascribed to
Madonna and Child with the Infant Baptist

POORTER, Willem de (1608–*c.* 1648)
An Allegorical Subject

PORDENONE, Giovanni Antonio (*c.* 1483–1539)
S. Bonaventure
S. Louis of Toulouse

PORDENONE, Giovanni Antonio ascribed to
Portrait of a Lady

PORTUGUESE School, first half of 16th century
The Mystic Marriage of S. Catherine

POT, Hendrick (*c.* 1585–1657)
A Merry Company at Table

POTTER, Paulus (1625–54)
A Landscape with Farm Animals
Cattle and Sheep in a stormy Landscape

POUSSIN, Nicolas (1594?–1665)
Bacchanalian Figures nurturing a Child
A Bacchanalian Revel before a Term of Pan
Cephalus and Aurora
The Annunciation
The Adoration of the Golden Calf **97**
Landscape with a Man killed by a Snake   **94**
The Adoration of the Shepherds
Landscape in the Roman Campagna with a Man scooping Water
Landscape in the Roman Campagna

POUSSIN, Nicolas (?)
Landscape: A Man washing his Feet at a Fountain

POUSSIN, Nicolas – after
Sleeping Nymph surprised by Satyrs
The Plague at Asdod

The Holy Family with SS. Elizabeth and John

POUSSIN, Nicolas – after (?)
Bacchanalian Festival (The Triumph of Silenus)

POUSSIN, Nicolas – follower of
Phineus and his Followers turned to Stone

POUSSIN, Nicolas – follower of (?)
Italian Landscape

POUSSIN, Pierre-Charles (1819–1904)
'Pardon Day in Brittany'

POZZOSERRATO, Ludovico (active 1581–1605) – ascribed to
Landscape with Mythological Figures
The Sons of Boreas pursuing the Harpies

PREDA, Giovanni Ambrogio (*c.* 1455–*c.* 1508)
Francesco di Bartolomeo Archinto (?)
Profile Portrait of a Lady

PRETI, Mattia (1613–99)
The Marriage at Cana

PREVITALI, Andrea (active 1502–28)
The Virgin and Child with a Donor
The Virgin and Child with SS. John the Baptist and Catherine
The Virgin and Child
Salvator Mundi
Salvator Mundi

Poussin: A Bacchanalian Revel before a Term of Pan

Raphael: An Allegory

Raphael: S. Catherine of Alexandria

Rembrandt: Equestrian Portrait

Rembrandt: Self-Portrait aged 34

Rembrandt: Margaretha de Geer

Reynolds: Anne, Countess
of Albemarle

Rosa: Self-Portrait

Rubens: The Judgment of Paris

Rubens: The Duke of Buckingham
conducted to the Temple of Virtus (?)

Ruisdael: A Waterfall

Ruysdael: A View of Rhenen
from the West

Saenredam: The Buurkerk at Utrecht

Scheffer: SS. Augustine and Monica

Sebastiano: Madonna and Child with SS. Joseph and John
the Baptist and a Donor

SEBASTIANO del Piombo
(c. 1485–1547)
The Raising of Lazarus
A Lady as S. Agatha
Madonna and Child with SS. Joseph
and John the Baptist and a Donor
The Daughter of Herodias

SEG(H)ERS, Hercules (1589–c.1633)
style of
A Mountainous Landscape

SEGNA di Bonaventura (active
1298–1331) – style of
Crucifix

SEISENEGGER, Jakob (1504–67)
Portrait of a Girl

SEURAT, Georges-Pierre (1859–91)
Bathers, Asnières   **168**

SHEE, Sir Martin Archer
(1769–1850)
W.T. Lewis as the Marquis in 'The
Midnight Hour'

SIBERECHTS, Joannes (1627–
c. 1703)
A Cowherd passing a Horse and Cart
in a Stream

SIENESE School, 14th century
The Marriage of the Virgin
S. Mary Magdalene
S. Peter

SIEVIER, Robert William
(1794–1865) – ascribed to
Wynn Ellis (marble bust)

Signorelli: Altarpiece:
The Circumcision

SIGNORELLI, Luca (1441?–1523)
Fresco: The Triumph of Chastity:
Love disarmed and bound
Altarpiece: The Circumcision
Altarpiece: The Adoration of the
Shepherds
The Adoration of the Shepherds
Altarpiece: The Virgin and Child
with Saints
The Holy Family
Fresco: Coriolanus persuaded by his
Family to spare Rome
Predella: Esther before Ahasuerus,
and three Visions of the Triumph of
S. Jerome

SISLEY, Alfred (1839–99)
The Horse Trough at Marly

SNIJDERS, Frans (1579–1657) –
follower of
Still Life of Fruit and Vegetables

SNIJERS, Peeter (1681–1752)
Still Life with dead Chickens and a
Lobster

SODOMA (1477–1549)
Madonna and Child with SS. Peter,
Catherine of Siena and a Carthusian
Donor
S. Jerome in Penitence

SODOMA – ascribed to
Madonna and Child
Head of Christ crowned with Thorns
bearing the Cross

SODOMA – follower of
The Nativity with the Infant Baptist
and Shepherds

SOGLIANI, Giovanni Antonio
(1492–1544)
Madonna and Child

SOLARI, Andrea (active
c. 1495–1524)
Giovanni Cristoforo Longoni
A Man with a Pink

SOLARI, Andrea – studio of
The Virgin and Child

SOLARIO, Antonio de (active
1502–18?)
S. Catherine of Alexandria
S. Ursula
The Virgin and Child with S. John

SOLIMENA, Francesco (1657–1747)
*Dido receiving Aeneas and Cupid
disguised as Ascanius*

SORGH, Hendrick (c. 1610–70)
*A Woman playing Cards with two
Boors*
Two Lovers at Table

SOUTH GERMAN School, 15th
century
S. John on Patmos

SOUTH GERMAN School, 16th
century
Portrait of a Man

SPAGNALO – (active 1504–28)
ascribed to
Christ crowned with Thorns
The Agony in the Garden
Christ at Gethsemane

SPANISH School, 17th century
Landscape with Figures

SPANISH School, 17th century
ascribed to
A Man, and a Child eating Grapes

SPINELLI, Giovanni Battista (?)
(?–c. 1647)
The Nativity

SPINELLO Aretino (active
1373–1411)
Fresco: Two Haloed Mourners
Fresco: S. Michael and Other Angels
Fresco: Decorative Border
Fresco: Decorative Border

SPRANGER, Bartholomaeus
(1546–1611)
The Adoration of the Kings

STANZIONE, Massimo (1585?–1656)
after
*Monks and Holy Women mourning
over the dead Christ*

STEEN, Jan (1625/6–79)
*A Young Woman playing a
Harpsichord*
Music making on a Terrace
*A Man blowing Smoke at a drunken
Woman*
A Pedlar selling Spectacles
Peasants merry-making outside an Inn
A Peasant Family at Meal-Time
A Man offering an Oyster to a Woman
Skittle Players outside an Inn

The Interior of an Inn

STEEN, Jan – after
An Itinerant Musician

STEENWYCK, Harmen (1612–
c. 1656)
*Still Life: An Allegory of the
Vanities of Human Life*

STEENWYCK II, Hendrick van
(c. 1580–c. 1649)
A Courtyard of a Renaissance Palace
The Interior of a Gothic Church

STEENWYCK II, Hendrick van, and
BRUEGEL, Jan I
The Interior of a Gothic Church
The Interior of a Gothic Church

STEENWYCK II, Hendrick van, and
a follower of BRUEGEL, Jan I
Croesus and Solon

STEENWYCK II, Hendrick van
imitator of
Interior of a Church at Night

STEVENS, Alfred (1823–1906)
Le Cadeau
Effet d'Orage à Honfleur

STORCK, Abraham (1644–c. 1704)
The Maas at Rotterdam

STROZZI, Bernardo (1581–1644)
A Personification of Fame

STUBBS, George (1724–1806)
*A Lady and a Gentleman in a
Carriage*
*The Milbanke and Melbourne
Families* **140**

SUBLEYRAS, Pierre (1699–1749)
after
The Bark of Charon

SUTTERMANS, Justus (1597–1681)
*The Grand Duke Ferdinand II of
Tuscany and his Wife Vittoria
della Rovere*

SUTTERMANS, Justus – ascribed to
Portrait of a Man

SWABIAN School, 15th century
*Portrait of a Woman of the Hofer
Family*

TACCONI, Francesco (active
1458–1500)
The Virgin and Child

Solari: Giovanni Cristoforo Longoni

Spranger: The Adoration of
the Kings

Steen: A Young Woman playing
a Harpsichord

Taillasson: Virgil reading the Aeneid to
Augustus and Octavia

Giovanni Domenico Tiepolo: The Deposition
from the Cross

Tintoretto: Christ washing his Disciples' Feet

Titian: Portrait of a Man

Titian: An Allegory of Prudence

Turner: Sun Rising Through Vapour: Fishermen
Cleaning and Selling Fish

Vallin: Dr. Forlenze

Ugolino: The Deposition

Van Gogh: A Cornfield, with Cypresses

Velázquez: The Immaculate Conception

Velázquez: S. John the Evangelist on
the Island of Patmos

Vermeer: A Young Woman seated
at a Virginal

Veronese: Adoration of the Kings

Vivarini: Panel
from an Altarpiece:
SS. Peter and Jerome

Vivarini: Panel
from an Altarpiece:
SS. Francis and Mark

VOET, Jakob Ferdinand
(1639–1700?)
Cardinal Carlo Cerri

VOUET, Simon (1590–1649)
Ceres and harvesting Cupids

VRIES, Adriaen de (c. 1560–1626)
after
Girl bathing (marble)

VRIES, Roelof van (1630–c. 1681)
A View of a Village

VROOM, Cornelis (c. 1590–1661)
*A Landscape with a River by a
Wood*

VUILLARD, Édouard (1868–1940)
The Chimneypiece
Lunch at Villeneuve-sur-Yonne (two
paintings)

WALSCAPPELLE, Jacob van
(1664–1727)
Flowers in a glass Vase

WATTEAU, Jean-Antoine
(1684–1721)
'La Gamme d'Amour'

WATTEAU, Jean-Antoine – after
'L'Accord Parfait'

WEENIX, Jan (1642?–1719)
*A Deer Hound with dead Game and
Implements of the Chase*

WEENIX, Jan Baptist (1621–60?)
*A Huntsman Cutting up a Dead
Deer, with Two Deerhounds*

WEIER, Jacob (active 1645–70)
Cavalry attacked by Infantry

WERFF, Adriaen van der
(1659–1722)
Portrait of a Man in a quilted Gown
A Boy with a Mouse Trap
The Rest on the Flight into Egypt

WET, the Elder, Jacob de (active
1633–c. 1675)
*A Landscape with a River at the Foot
of a Hill*

WEYDEN, Rogier van der
(c. 1399–1464)
The Magdalen reading

Follower of Verrocchio: Tobias and the Angel

55   Vouet: Ceres and harvesting Cupids

Van der Weyden: Portrait of a Lady

Van der Weyden: S. Ivo (?)